Rugged and Enduring

Rugged and Enduring

The Eagles, The Browns, and 5 Years of Football

David Cohen

Cover Photo is of Philadelphia's Al Wistert

Library of Congress Number:		2001119179
ISBN #:	Hardcover	1-4010-2183-2
	Softcover	1-4010-2182-4

This book was printed in the United States of America.

To order additional copies of this book, contact:

Xlibris Corporation

1-888-7-XLIBRIS

www.Xlibris.com

Orders@Xlibris.com

Contents

In memory of Albert Franklin Cohen (1932-1987).
My father was a Philadelphia Eagles fan.

INTRODUCTION

Football's history is missing. The great names of its distant past are just that, names, conjuring up no particular images to most fans. This is particularly true of those men who played professionally before television and the Super Bowl brought the game into the living rooms of many millions of Americans. Change has been a constant of the sport, and the game that was played in the NFL's first four decades is just too different from today's game for routine comparisons to be made.

This book is meant to provide some context for the NFL today. It examines the sport from 1941 to 1960, with an in-depth look at five key seasons in the history of professional football, 1946 to 1950. That period began with a postwar boom that lifted the sport to new heights; it ended with a merger of two pro leagues and the most dramatic season that the NFL had ever seen. Those years also saw the integration of the sport, the spread of pro football to the West Coast, the use of new and revived strategies that made the sport more exciting, the arrival of television, and the single most important rule change in the sport's history, one that permitted players to enter and leave a game at any time. In a sport that puts great emphasis on progress, on coming up with bigger, faster and stronger players and new plays that no one will be able to stop, this was an era of unprecedented growth.

The changes that took place from 1946 to 1950 did not in and of themselves boost pro football to the sport that it has become. There was no single defining great moment on par with the 1958 Giants-

Colts championship game or Joe Namath's guarantee of victory in Super Bowl III that caused the nation to stand up and take notice. But the events and achievements of these years moved forward professional football, setting it up for a grand future. This book is a chronicle of that time.

"Rugged and Enduring" is intended not only to celebrate the players and coaches of this era for how they pushed the NFL down the road to change, but also to celebrate their accomplishments. This is their story: Where they came from, how they lived, how they played, why they played, what they achieved. Fifty-six former players have helped me by sharing their observations on their game. Their recollections and comments are sprinkled throughout the text.

*****

It was the middle of September 1950 and the defending champion Philadelphia Eagles were preparing to open their National Football League season. So were the defending champion Cleveland Browns. They were facing each other in Philadelphia and the outcome of this unique game–the first in NFL history to match two defending champions–would go a long way toward determining the future of the NFL.

The Cleveland Browns had last played in December when they beat the San Francisco 49ers to win their fourth consecutive championship in the upstart All-America Football Conference (AAFC). That same month, the NFL absorbed the Baltimore Colts, 49ers, and Browns from the 4-year-old league in a long-awaited merger. Even before the merger, the pundits had been itching to see how the Browns would do against the NFL's best. Paul Brown, Cleveland's coach and the man for whom the team was named, kept saying that his squad could play with anybody.

The Philadelphia Eagles weren't particularly worried. Coached by Greasy Neale, this veteran squad had posted back-to-back shutouts in the last two NFL championship games, a feat no other team had ever accomplished. Like many of their brethren in the NFL, they were used to looking down upon the Browns.

"The paper from Philadelphia," recalled Browns quarterback Otto Graham, one of the stars of the defunct league, "sent a reporter into our camp. And he was in our camp for five or six weeks. And he kept sending reports back, articles and so forth, 'Hey people in Philadelphia. You better be prepared. This is a good football team, you know.' Everybody thought he was trying to build up the game."

Graham and his teammates were used to this by now. Since 1946, NFL insiders have been taking shots at them, and Paul Brown have been posting the clippings in their locker room. Despite their dominance in the AAFC and a bevy of stars–Graham, fullback Marion Motley, ends Dante Lavelli and Mac Speedie, kicker-tackle Lou Groza, linemen Bill Willis and Len Ford–few seemed willing to believe that they had the talent to match up in the more-established league.

NFL insiders also had doubts about Paul Brown and his system. A firm believer in discipline, unity and preparation, Brown treated football like a science, bringing a studious approach to the game that went way beyond that of Greasy Neale and other top coaches. And despite the presence of Motley, a steamroller in the backfield, Brown loved to pass the ball, using precision passing routes. The Eagles had made good use of the pass over the years, but they thought Brown and the Browns had gone too far.

"Greasy wouldn't go and see, he wouldn't go and see the Browns play!" recalled Eagles tackle Al Wistert, one of the team's leaders. "I went to see them play, because I hurt my knee and while my knee was injured, I went to Cleveland and watched the Browns. Then when you'd come back and tell him some things that they were doing, he would say, 'Well they can't do that against us. They'll never do that against us. They can't do that' because he was very proud of his football team. We had a very excellent football team."

A blustery character not above going to the racetrack with his players, Neale had reason to have faith in his team. They had played in three consecutive NFL title games, shutting out a Rams team with a similarly high-flying pass offense in the 1949 game. His Eagles could match the Browns virtually star for star: quarterback Tommy Thompson, ends Pete Pihos and Jack Ferrante, and a first-rate collection of linemen that included Wistert, Vic Lindskog, Alex Wojciechowicz, Vic Sears, Frank "Bucko" Kilroy, and second-year player Chuck Bednarik.

Neale had virtually unlimited faith in his meal ticket, running back Steve Van Buren, who had scored the only touchdown in the 1948 championship game and rushed for a record 196 yards in the 1949 title game. And Neale was no slouch in the strategy department, having created a 5-2-4 defense that had changed the way defense was played.

Still, there was reason to think this could be a close game. The Browns were surprisingly successful in the exhibition season, even beating George Halas' Chicago Bears. The favored Eagles suddenly found themselves without Van Buren, Wistert and halfback Bosh Pritchard, all of whom were banged up. And the weather was cooperating, something it never did for Neale's Eagles. In the 1947 title game vs. the Cardinals, they had been forced to play on a frozen field. The next year, these teams played a rematch in a blizzard. Against Los Angeles in the 1949 title game, there was a relentless rain. Here it was, a big game, and the weather was, well, perfectly fine. This was quite unexpected.

On Sept. 16, more than 60 of the world's top football players took the field in Philadelphia's packed Municipal Stadium. One of the most memorable confrontations in league history was about to take place, a game that players from both teams would remember vividly for decades and decades. What follows is the story of that game–as well as many of the games that led up to it and some of the ones that followed it.

1

GREASY & DIRTY

****

The Sunday that Pearl Harbor was bombed, three National Football League games were played. Dec. 7, 1941, was the last day of the NFL schedule. Four teams had already completed their schedules: Pro games were then scheduled much like college contests were, with teams starting and ending their seasons whenever it suited them. Most games were played on Sunday, but teams also played weekday or Saturday games when a baseball team was using their ballpark on Sunday.

On that Sunday, the two New York City teams, the Giants and the Dodgers, were playing at the Polo Grounds; and the two Chicago teams, the Bears and the Cardinals, were playing at Comiskey Park. The Giants had already won the Eastern Division, but George Halas' Bears needed a victory over the Cardinals to force a divisional playoff with Curly Lambeau's Green Bay Packers. The Bears, trying to become the first NFL team to win back-to-back titles, got the victory. They went on to beat Green Bay and then defeat the Giants for the title–though, by that time, World War II had so preoccupied America that almost nobody showed up for the championship game.

The only game on Dec. 7 that involved teams from different cities pitted Washington against Philadelphia in the nation's capital. That city was soon to have much else to worry about, but, as it was, attendance was only 27,102. George Preston Marshall's Redskins, despite the pres-

11403-COHE

ence of brilliant passer Sammy Baugh, were closing out a disappointing season. After winning the East in 1940, Washington was staggering along at 5-5. And while there were some outstanding opposing players who might draw Washington fans out to see a meaningless December game–Green Bay end Don Hutson or, perhaps, Bears stars Sid Luckman and George McAfee–the Eagles did not possess any of them. Philadelphia had not beaten Washington since 1937, and the team was about to complete its ninth consecutive losing season. If they were to beat the Redskins, they would finish the season with more than two wins for only the fourth time in their history. They did not.

But it was not as if the Eagles, playing under rookie Coach Earle "Greasy" Neale, had quit. The previous week, for instance, the Eagles had added a back, Jack Hinkle. Hinkle had played in 1940 for the Giants. After a dispute with Coach Steve Owen, he jumped to the New York Americans of the fledgling American Football League for the 1941 season, playing in a backfield with 1940 Heisman Trophy winner Tom Harmon and Jarrin' John Kimbrough, the Heisman runner-up. By December, the AFL's season had concluded, so Philadelphia GM Harry Thayer called Hinkle and asked if he would like to join the Eagles for their final game. At first, Hinkle recounted, he was reluctant: "Well, I had played so damn much football–you know, in those days, you played 60 minutes, 58-60 minutes–and I was fed right up to the ears with it." But the $300 that Thayer offered was sorely tempting, so Hinkle agreed, provided that Thayer could guarantee that the back would be allowed to rejoin the Americans in 1942. He was assured that he could.

Hinkle would be good enough to play professionally for five more seasons, but his presence on this day didn't turn the tide. Baugh threw two fourth-quarter touchdown passes and Washington won, 20-14. All accounts indicate that owner George Preston Marshall, citing a policy against broadcasting non-sports news, declined to allow news of the attack on Pearl Harbor to be announced over the public address system. But the news trickled in to those in the stands listening on radios, and the stadium rapidly started emptying out as many of those in the stands found themselves being paged and told to report to their offices.

Thayer's guarantee to Jack Hinkle did not turn out to mean much:

The American Football League ceased to exist before the 1942 season. And like many, many professional athletes, Hinkle found himself in the U.S. military soon after the Pearl Harbor attack. By the time most of these men returned, pro football was ready to take a giant step forward.

*****

By the Forties, people had been getting paid to play football for just about 50 years. The first professionals were college heroes who were imported by local teams to enhance their chances against a single opponent or a slate of opponents. It didn't take many years for fully pro teams to emerge. In time, regional rivalries emerged, particularly in the mining regions of Ohio and Pennsylvania, paving the way for the first of what we think of as pro leagues.

At this time, pro football was not at all reputable. In the early part of this century going from college football to pro football was roughly the equivalent of going from amateur wrestling to professional wrestling today, except that no one seriously worries about the reputation of amateur wrestling being stained by whatever association it might have with the pros. But back then, college football coaches such as Amos Alonzo Stagg saw their players playing for them on Saturdays and then playing for a pro team on Sundays, and branded the pros as a menace to their way of life.

The first professional rivalry of note involved the Ohio communities of Massillon and Canton. In 1906, the coach of the Canton Bulldogs, Blondy Wallace, was accused of having bribed one of his own players to lose a game to the Massillon team, setting back both the rivalry and the sport. Nine years later, things picked up again between the two cities when Canton signed Jim Thorpe, already a legend for his performance in the 1912 Olympics and his gridiron heroics for a Pennsylvania college, Carlisle. Massillon had such notables as Notre Dame stars Knute Rockne and Gus Dorais, and both teams had an assortment of other college stars playing under assumed names. Their big game that year ended when a fan, standing in the end zone in a standing room only section, knocked the ball out of the hands of a

Massillon player who apparently had scored the game-tying touchdown. The officials, afraid to make a ruling on the play in front of such an unruly mob, left their decision (they decided that it was not a touchdown) in an envelope at a local hotel and high-tailed it out of town before the envelope could be opened. It was hardly the stuff of Harvard-Yale or Army-Navy.

In 1920, Canton went on to become a charter member of the American Professional Football Conference, which was renamed the National Football League in 1922. At this time, there wasn't much reason to think that this league would be more stable, durable, or important than any of the loose bands of pro teams to be found anywhere. Fourteen teams played in the league that first year, most of them from the Midwest. The Muncie Flyers played only one game and lost it, while the Decatur Staleys played 13, winning 10 and tying two. The Akron Pros were awarded the title after winning eight games and tying their other three. In 1922, the Staleys moved to Chicago and became the Bears. With George Halas already at the helm, the Bears were set for a long and storied history. By 1922, the league also included the Green Bay Packers, which remains the oldest one-city franchise in the sport.

The idea behind this circuit was to ensure some stability: Teams were constantly bidding against each other for players who jumped back and forth, sometimes playing for more than one team at the same time. There is a story, perhaps apocryphal, of a player who said that he played against Knute Rockne six weeks in a row–Rockne was playing on six different teams. But the early NFL was anything but stable: Teams were born, teams moved, teams died.

The league was home to such franchises as the 1922-23 Oorang Indians, composed entirely of Indians. The team was owned by a man named Walter Lingo; his primary interest in owning the team was promoting the sale of Airedales that he bred. Jim Thorpe and fellow Hall-of-Famer Joe Guyon were the team's stars, but their games were secondary to the team's halftime shows, which featured the canines displaying their talents, as well as Indian dances and wrestling matches between one of the players and a bear. The team, not surprisingly, was a dog.

Fritz Pollard, John M. Carroll's biography of the NFL's first black quarterback and its first black coach, paints the pro football of the Twenties in a less-than-shining light. Gambling and football went hand-in-hand, and there appears to have been little in the way of ethics or loyalty. The games were often ugly, either low-scoring (or scoreless) affairs with an emphasis on line play and pileups, or blowouts pitting one solid franchise against a collection of stragglers. Even at its best, the early pro game was a game of field position, where a vital offensive weapon was the "quick kick"–a play where someone in the backfield would unexpectedly punt the ball away with the expectation that his team's defense would bottle up their opponents and they would get the ball back in better position. The best offense, as they say, was thought to be a good defense.

Pollard, one of the more gifted players of the time, was constantly changing teams, playing for one team while coaching another, all while trying to coach college or high school teams or both. He was far from the league's only nomad; one of the league's most gifted players and notorious wild men, Johnny Blood, even was nicknamed "The Vagabond Halfback." Some teams represented a certain city in name only–there was a Los Angeles team in the NFL in 1926 but it never had a home game. And the notion of pro football as a collection of greedy nomads only grew after University of Illinois legend Harold "Red" Grange was signed to a contract in 1925 and "The Galloping Ghost" was sent out on a barnstorming tour with the Chicago Bears. Halas' heroes played just about any team they could find.

Though Grange's tour broke all sorts of attendance records, it also showcased the game in just about the worst possible light, as some sort of dubious spectacle rather than as a serious team sport. It soon became obvious that the sport had not retained the interest of those attracted by the novelty of the heralded tour. In 1926, Grange and promoter C.C. (his nickname was "Cash-and-Carry") Pyle tried to use Grange's fame to launch a new league. This American Football League lasted one year. Also in 1926, the NFL's ailing Duluth franchise signed college superstar Ernie Nevers and sent the team out on tour. The Duluth Eskimos did well for one year, but the franchise expired after the 1927 season. In an era of unmatched prosperity for baseball, boxing, and other forms of entertainment, football grew spasmodically.

These barnstorming tours did nothing to change the impression that pro football was considerably less spirited and less pure than college football. At this time, turning pro was seen as a betrayal of the higher ideals of college ball; the Big Ten conference even adopted a rule requiring that former college players who turned pro be asked to return their varsity letters. In 1932, Grange, who had settled in for a quality stretch with the Bears, went so far as to co-write an article for The Saturday Evening Post entitled "The College Game Is Easier." The tone of the article indicates that Grange was doing his damnedest to convince a skeptical public that pro football was a worthy endeavor.

By the early 1930s, Grange had been joined in the pros by such other stars as Bronko Nagurski, but it was still presumed that it was college that set the standard for what football was–and what it should be. Two years later, when an annual all-star game between the NFL champion and a team of college all-stars was launched, it was not assumed, as it would be in later years, that this game inherently favored the pros. "A pro game is motion," said Bob Zuppke, Grange's coach at Illinois, in an oft-repeated remark. "A college game is emotion."

The NFL took its first step forward in 1933. By then, big cities had, for the most part, replaced the little Pennsylvania and Ohio towns where the league had started. In the early years, the champion was chosen by a vote at the league meetings; it was as imprecise a method as the way that champions were chosen in college football. In 1933, the NFL was split into two divisions, allowing for a championship game to be played. The league also made the game different from the college one in a number of ways, making it easier to pass the ball. This was the first time that the NFL had officially differentiated itself from the college game. The next year, however, the league was still averaging a mere 8,211 fans per game. College attendance figures from those years are hard to come by, but there is considerable anecdotal evidence that some college teams drew more fans per game than the pros drew per season.

1933 was also the year that the NFL emulated baseball by drawing a color line. No policy was ever announced; no official end to the practice of hiring black players was ever disclosed. But until 1933, there had been some black players in the league, including such stars as Fritz Pollard and Duke Slater, and after 1933, there were none. In later years, Bears patriarch George Halas was often quoted as saying that there never was a policy barring blacks, it was just that no blacks were good enough to play in the league after 1933. Given the caliber of black players available in the Thirties–Ozzie Simmons of the University of Iowa; Brud Holland of Cornell; and Woody Strode, Kenny Washington and Jackie Robinson of UCLA–few people have ever believed him.

As the Thirties went on, the league grew more stable, but it still found it tough to buy respectability. Today it is pretty much a given that a college football star will join the pros after his collegiate days; the only exceptions are people committed to military service and some two-sport athletes. There is an underlying assumption that all red-blooded young men dream of playing in the NFL. But in the Thirties and early Forties, there were a number of certified immortals who declined to turn pro.

The best known is Jay Berwanger, the University of Chicago back who was the first winner of the Heisman Trophy and the first selection in the inaugural NFL draft. Declining to turn pro only seems to have enhanced his considerable college legend.

Berwanger was not alone: The next two Heisman Trophy winners, Yale stars Larry Kelley and Clint Frank, also declined to turn pro, while a standout University of Michigan center named Gerald Ford picked law school over offers from George Halas and Curly Lambeau and wound up president of these United States. Of the 14 players listed in the NCAA record book as having being named all-American in 1935, six (Larry Lutz, John Weller, Gomer Jones, J.C. Wetsel, Bobby Grayson, and Berwanger) do not appear in the NFL encyclopedia as having played in the league.

And some players consented to join the NFL only for a year or two, acting as if the league were something on the order of a post-graduation trip to Europe to be enjoyed before embarking on graduate school or a real career. One of the decade's best backs, Byron "Whizzer" White, at first declined to turn pro, but was coaxed into playing in 1938 before he headed off to Oxford and Yale Law School. He returned to the NFL for the 1940 and 1941 seasons only when he was told that he could attend law school while he played. White wound up serving three decades on the U.S. Supreme Court.

Davey O'Brien, a worthy successor to Sammy Baugh at Texas Christian and the 1938 Heisman Trophy winner, played only two seasons in the NFL. In the last game of 1940, he completed 33 of 60 passes for 316 yards and one touchdown in an aerial duel with Baugh. His performance set league records; the last of his Philadelphia Eagles team records was not broken until 1989. After that game, however, O'Brien left football for a career in the FBI. College football now honors its best quarterback every year with an award bearing O'Brien's name.

Even people who really didn't have much else to do abandoned the league rather routinely. In *The Pro Football Chronicle*, Dan Daly & Bob O'Donnell describe how Gaynell Tinsley, a gifted end for the Cardinals in 1937-38, retired in 1939 because of some disputes with the management and Coach Ernie Nevers. Tinsley came back in 1940 for one lackluster season and then left the pro game behind for good. A paroled felon by the name of Alabama Pitts joined the Eagles for four games in 1935. Pitts, the only player listed in Philadelphia's media guide as an alumnus of Sing Sing, subsequently turned down an offer of $50 per game to stick around and left the league.

There were other players, of course, who spent many years in the NFL: College stars Sammy Baugh, Sid Luckman, and Alex Wojciechowicz played professionally until 1950 and beyond. Today, pro sports are so lucrative that it's very hard for a gifted athlete to kiss them off at age 22 or 24; in the 1930s, it was not all that hard to turn one's back on the NFL. The league's million-dollar contracts were a long way off.

"In 1942, when I was drafted by the Pittsburgh Steelers as the No.

1 draft choice," recounted NFL Hall of Famer Bill Dudley, "the first thing I remember was the equipment they had was not as good as we had at college. I brought my own shoulder pads, hip pads, and helmet because I had such a small head . . . they didn't have one in camp that would fit."

"Practically all the games that the pros played," Dudley continued, "were in baseball parks, and Forbes Field, home of the Pittsburgh Pirates, was no exception. There was no attempt to re-grass the infield or anything like that and the pitcher's mound was cut down, but never level with the field."

The coming of World War II also put a strain on the league. To keep up morale on the homefront, President Franklin Delano Roosevelt had allowed sports to continue, but the war took a toll on football, depleting the existing talent and reducing the number of young players coming into the leagues. Even those athletes who did not enlist often spent their weeks working in war industries, sometimes in other cities, joining their teams only on nights or the weekend.

While some football players excelled during the war years–Green Bay end Don Hutson had the best years of a great career during World War II–the game fought to survive. The third incarnation of the American Football League, born in 1940 and featuring the memorably named Columbus Bullies, ceased to exist after the 1941 season. In the NFL, the schedule was shortened from 11 games to 10 from 1943 to 1945. The Cleveland Rams did not field a team in 1943, while the Pittsburgh Steelers and Philadelphia Eagles merged for that season, playing as the Steagles. Cleveland and Philadelphia returned in 1944, but the Steelers combined with the Chicago Cardinals, playing one awful 0-10 season dubbed the Carpets. In 1945, the Boston Yanks and Brooklyn Tigers merged. The idea of keeping the home fires burning lost some of its luster as teams surrendered their identities and became a combination of friend and foe.

And with the NFL not being the most respectable organization in the world, there were plenty of players who had no qualms about leaving their sport and finding some kind of serious way to contribute to the war effort. Take, for example, the case of Leon Cook, a tackle from Northwestern.

After being rejected by the draft board because of bad eyes and a bad knee, Cook initially turned down the Philadelphia Eagles in 1942 for a job with a chemical firm in Buffalo. When he concluded that he was contributing far less to the war effort in that position than he had hoped, he joined the Eagles–becoming a reserve tackle behind Vic Sears–and tried anew to get in the military. Again, he was unsuccessful. Then, Cook recalled, "I began searching for a job that would be of value to the war effort and was hired by Du Pont in the High Explosive Laboratory at Gibbstown, N.J." That ended his football career.

"My high-explosive research was quite gratifying," Cook said. "I finally felt that I was doing the right thing to help my many friends overseas." It was the kind of decision that young men made in those days without hesitation or regret.

*****

One thing, perhaps the only thing, that the pros did have going for them all those years was the caliber of their coaching. There is little doubt that the best of these men made the most out of a game that could easily degenerate into what seemed like a series of senseless collisions. These were men of imagination and daring, men who thought that if they worked at the chalkboard long enough, they'd come up with a new wrinkle that nobody had ever seen before–and nobody would be able to stop.

The towering figures of the early years of pro football were Steve Owen of the Giants, Ray Flaherty of the Redskins, Curly Lambeau of the Packers, and the giant of them all, George Halas of the Bears, the man whose T-formation offense demolished the Redskins, 73-0, in the 1940 championship game. Having a good coach was the biggest thing separating the NFL's good teams from its lousy ones. It was with that in mind that the Eagles, after three years under Lud Wray (9 wins, 21 losses, 1 tie) and five under Bert Bell (10-44-2), turned to the colorful, blustery Earle "Greasy" Neale in 1941.

At the time, Neale had neither coached nor played in the NFL. In fact, truth be told, football wasn't even his favorite sport. "My first love was baseball, and my consuming ambition was to become a big leaguer. The football I played as a youngster was merely a fill-in to keep busy until it was warm enough for baseball," he was quoted as saying in 1951. But by the end of his tenure, no one with the Eagles could have possibly regretted hiring Neale.

Neale was born in Parkersburg, W. Va., on Nov. 5, 1891. His nickname, the New York Times said at the time of his death, dated from his boyhood days: A neighborhood child, whom he dubbed "Dirty," retaliated by calling him "Greasy." In high school, he made his coaching debut as a player-coach–after the coach resigned, Neale was named to replace him.

When Neale graduated, he went to West Virginia Wesleyan, where he played end and halfback. Legend has it that he caught 14 passes in a row during the tiny school's astonishing 19-14 upset of the University of West Virginia in 1912. (This was a year before the Notre Dame tandem of Gus Dorais and Knute Rockne are supposed to have made throwing the football fashionable.) At college, he also met and married Genevieve Horne.

According to writer Jack Cusack, Neale then joined the Canton Bulldogs and played in Canton's big games against Massillon. Neale played under the name of Fisher, and accounts of that season depict him as a standout for a star-studded team that included the likes of Jim Thorpe. John Kellison, who joined Canton at the same time, worked under Neale for many years, including all of Neale's seasons with Philadelphia. (Tackle Vic Sears observed many years later that Kellison was the perfect complement to the blustery Neale because he appeared to have no ego whatsoever.)

Even as he was playing for Canton, Neale was establishing himself in pro baseball. He played for the Cincinnati Reds from 1916 to 1922, with a brief detour in Philadelphia in 1921 and a three-game stint back with the Reds in 1924. In 1917, his best year, he hit .294 as he shared outfield duties with Hall of Famer Edd Roush and the multi-talented Jim Thorpe. In the 1919 World Series, the series intentionally lost by the infamous Black Sox of Chicago, Neale hit .357 with a team-leading 10 hits for the victorious Reds. In 1928, he spent a year as third-base coach of the St. Louis Cardinals.

Around the time he joined the Reds, Neale also moved into the coaching ranks in college football. His first job as a head coach was at Muskingum in New Concord, Ohio, in 1915. He returned to West Virginia Wesleyan to coach in 1916-1917, then moved on to Marietta. In 1921, he made his reputation as a strategic wizard when he led Washington and Jefferson University to the 1922 Rose Bowl, where they played the University of California to a 0-0 tie. Given that the California squads of those years were known as the "Wonder Teams" and were in the middle of a 50-game unbeaten streak, holding them to a tie was a stupendous accomplishment. It was the highlight of Neale's collegiate coaching career.

Neale's gridiron coaching career would also take him to the University of Virginia (where he was head coach from 1923 to 1928), the semipro Ironton Tanks (1930), West Virginia (head coach 1931-33) and Yale, where he was the backfield coach under Raymond "Ducky" Pond from 1934 to 1940. In 1941, steel tycoon Alexis Thompson hired Neale to coach the Eagles. Thompson, a Yale alum who had swapped ownership of the Pittsburgh Steelers to Art Rooney and Bert Bell for the Eagles earlier that year, was operating on the recommendation of Giants coach Steve Owen, Neale's longtime friend.

In recent years, so many coaches have copied the gentlemanly and aloof style of Paul Brown and Tom Landry that it has come to be the norm for NFL head coaches; blustery characters such as Jerry Glanville and Buddy Ryan are treated as the exceptions. In the early Forties, this was not the case. Greasy Neale was decidedly vulgar: When Yale hired him as an assistant, officials of the school asked sports reporters to refrain from using his nickname. But Neale told newsmen, "Yale or no Yale, if you fellows want to call me Greasy, go ahead."

Neale's behavior often shocked newcomers to the Eagles. Tackle Al Wistert told writer Ray Didinger: "My first impression of Greasy Neale was he was the most uncouth man I ever met. He cussed and swore. . . . I wasn't used to that." Leon Cook noted that the most memorable thing about his short stay with the Eagles was the "cultural shock" caused by the difference in style between gentlemanly Northwestern coach Lynn "Pappy" Waldorf and Neale.

But, players who stuck with Neale came to realize that the coach was no blowhard. Neale had an encyclopedic mind, and players noted that he remembered just about every play he had ever seen, in detail. They say he was constantly running through what amounted to a whole history of the game every time he planned strategy.

"He was a very knowledgeable coach and a highly intelligent guy," recalled Wistert, who joined the team in 1943 and stayed with Neale for the rest of his career. "For instance, he was an excellent bridge player. And he could, when a bridge hand was over, he could reconstruct the whole thing and play the whole hand all over again verbally. Show you what mistakes you made. It was just amazing what a mind that man had."

On the field, Neale demanded absolute precision. Almost every one of Neale's players remembered some point at which they became exasperated by his criticism as he made them practice the same play over and over until they executed it exactly to his liking.

"He was very pronounced, and very strict on what he did. Everything had to be exactly right," recalled end Dick Humbert, who was a rookie in Neale's first year. "He would run a play 50 times and each time it would look like it was run the same, but he'd criticize it, said it was here or there, change it until it was run right. So he was a very, very tenacious coach . . . He just had to have things exactly right."

As exasperating as he could be, Neale commanded the respect of his players. For one thing, he respected them, particularly his veterans, enough to accept input from them on the playing field.

"Newcomers to the team," said an article in a 1949 Eagles game program, "are amazed and sometimes shocked when they hear players argue with Coach Neale on the practice field. They can't get over it. As a matter of fact, Greasy encourages players to discuss everything with him. 'A coach doesn't know everything and these players have minds of their own. I see no reason why they can't express themselves on the practice field. In fact I like it.'"

1403-COHE

Still, Neale was clearly the boss–a very demanding one–on the field. Off the field, everything was different. Simply put, Neale placed himself on the same level as his players.

"He wanted to be close to his players," Al Wistert recalled. "He and his wife, Genevieve, both were always with the players. They did not hold themselves aloof from the players as so many coaches do." Ernie Steele, a back who joined the squad in 1942, says that he and Greasy "roomed right across from each other in the hotel. . . . His wife and my wife were very close."

Wistert and other players remembered coaxing Neale into canceling afternoon practices during training camp–provided, of course, the team did everything perfectly in the morning practice–so Neale and others could play golf. Neale also shared an affinity with some of his players for betting on horses, and he would sit with his athletes on train rides, playing gin and pinochle.

Steele recalled going out the night before games with Neale and sitting around and talking with him. Steele wouldn't drink because it was the night before a game, but Neale would have a few beers as they chatted. "When the day arrives that I can't associate with my players," Neale was quoted as saying in a 1949 Eagles game program, "that will be the day when I quit coaching." In essence, Neale was able to build a basic trust with the team, an understanding that in exchange for their top effort at times when he absolutely had to be in command, they could have his friendship off the field.

"Greasy was, well, he played golf with the guys, you know. He would play cards with 'em. And he was friendly that way," Dick Humbert recalled.

"He'd come to your house and have dinner with you and your family, but the next day on the field, why, you wouldn't think he even knew you," laughed Humbert. "I mean, he was two different people, as a friend, fine; but when you were playing ball for him, it was all business and that's the way it should be."

The complex nature of Neale's relationship with his players is perhaps one reason for one of his most distinctive traits: A marked fondness for veterans at the expense of rookies. Throughout his tenure with the Eagles, Neale consistently expressed disdain for his youngest players.

"I remember when he first came with the ballclub," recounted Jack Hinkle. "He said, 'Give me a team of veterans and I'll win championships.'

"Your first year," Hinkle added, "you didn't particularly have any fondness for him. But your second you started to love the guy. And then as each year went by, you loved him much more."

But when Neale first came to the Eagles in 1941, he had little in the way of able veterans–or able players of any kind. Star passer Davey O'Brien, the best player on the dismal 1940 team that had won only one game for Bert Bell, had retired. When Neale took the helm, he oversaw the departure of many of the other members of that team. He then went scrounging for talent anywhere he could find it.

"When Greasy Neale took over the team, whatever he had left from the old Eagles, then whatever he could grab from the teams that released ballplayers, he took in, " recounted end Jack Ferrante, who joined the team in 1941. Still, Neale's revamped squad managed only two wins and a tie that first year. In 1942, the team was substantially made over again, this time because a number of players had enlisted in the military. That squad also won only two games. The Eagles had never been much of a gate attraction–in 1937, they drew 23,698 fans for five home games–and they were still not drawing well. They were unable to attract more than 15,500 fans for any of their 1942 home games at Shibe Park on Philadelphia's north side.

In 1943, the franchise suffered a further indignity: It was combined with the Pittsburgh Steelers and spent the year as the Steagles. Neale became co-coach with Walt Kiesling and found himself in a situation in which only half the players would listen to him.

"The coaches didn't get along," recalled back Ernie Steele, who was coming down from his service post in New York to play each weekend. "Both coaches wanted to be the head honcho. The ballplayers, they were listening to their coach and not listening to the other coach." Jack Hinkle, who had returned to the team after being kept away by military duty in 1942, remembered a time when Kiesling pulled his players off the field after a disagreement between Neale and one of the Steelers.

If the notion of dueling coaches wasn't bad enough, the best players on each team, Eagles quarterback Tommy Thompson and Pittsburgh back Bill Dudley, went into the service before the 1943 season, leaving the team without direction. The team was without lots of other things as well.

"Equipment was scarce," Dan Rooney, son of Art Rooney, told writer Alan Robinson in 1993. "We kept it in the basement of our house so we didn't lose it. Cleats were really hard to get because they were rubber product."

Worst of all for the Eagles was that the Steelers were basically no good either. In fact, Pittsburgh was just about the only team that Philadelphia had beaten regularly in its first decade of existence. "The only trouble," with the 1943 team, recalled Al Wistert, "was that they had twice as many lousy players that season."

But somehow Neale and Kiesling managed to give new life to two struggling franchises, coaxing five victories out of this team to give the Philadelphia franchise its first winning season (5-4-1). Roy Zimmerman, who had been acquired from Washington, was the starting quarterback, while Jack Hinkle came within two yards of leading the NFL in rushing. The team even made a run at the division title.

And, when Philadelphia and Pittsburgh split up after that season, it became apparent that Neale had assembled a fine collection of linemen for the Eagles. Vic Sears, Al Wistert, Frank "Bucko" Kilroy, Bruno Banducci and Vic Lindskog all would be good enough to play professionally at least through 1951, and all would be named to the All-Pro team at least once. As a group, they began to emerge in 1944.

1944 also saw the arrival of a bashful rookie runner from Louisiana State University who made the Eagles a force to be reckoned with. Steve Van Buren, who had been kept out of the military by a chronic eye ailment, recalled that he had never actually *heard of* the Philadelphia Eagles until they drafted him. But, in Van Buren's rookie season, Neale's Eagles were seriously in the hunt for the title for the first time, going unbeaten for the first seven weeks and ultimately posting a mark of 7-

1-2 to finish on the heels of Steve Owen's 8-1-1 Giants. Van Buren, Zimmerman, and Wistert were named All-Pro.

In 1945, the Eagles finished second at 7-3, one game behind Washington. Van Buren scored a record-setting 110 points in 1945, more than the Eagles had scored in 1933, 1935, 1936, 1937 or 1939, and more than either the Steelers or Cardinals scored that season. They even beat the Cleveland Rams, the eventual league champions, 28-14. Van Buren and Wistert were named All-Pro again, and the team drew some record-setting crowds.

Even so, there were some doubts as to how good Neale's team really was–with so many players in the service during those years, the caliber of competition in the NFL was clearly not what it once was. With the end of World War II, Neale and his team were going to have to prove in 1946 that their success was not a fluke.

2

1946—NEW STARTS & NEW STRATEGY

****

The Philadelphia Eagles opened the 1946 season on Sept. 29 in Los Angeles. This was the first regular-season NFL game played on the West Coast. The Eagles were the first home opponent of the Rams, a franchise that had moved west from Cleveland after winning the 1945 NFL title on the strength of the passing arm and athleticism of rookie Bob Waterfield.

The move west seemed to suit the Rams, a team which had a certain glamour about it. In fact, Waterfield was already married to movie star Jane Russell, his high school sweetheart. But having to play thousands of miles from home left Greasy Neale a little baffled. This, after all, involved a time difference of three hours and a significant climate change.

"Greasy brought us out there a week ahead of time," recalled Allie Sherman, Eagles backup quarterback. "In those days, nobody knew–well, everybody had ideas, the time zone changes, and how do you handle it and so on–and he thought he'd take us out there for a week ahead of time. And, we'd get acclimated and so on. Well, that was true in a way, but that also came at the same time that smog, the industrial smog, and the environment of Los Angeles, started to appear. We were working out there during the week, and . . . we'd work and our eyes would tear and we'd cough.

"Game day, the temperature down on the floor of the Coliseum was 108 degrees. There had been a heat wave, you know, one of those major heat waves you have throughout the country at times, people dying in the Southwest and the Midwest, things like that."

Besides being the first league game on the West Coast, the game was a milestone in another regard. This was to be the first time since 1933 that the Eagles, or anybody else in the NFL for that matter, had played against an integrated team. The Rams had signed two black players, a pair of local stars from UCLA, back Kenny Washington and end Woody Strode. In the second half, Waterfield tore a rib muscle and Washington took over briefly at quarterback, completing a 19-yard pass to All-Pro end Jim Benton. But it was Waterfield and company that did the damage as the Rams outplayed the Eagles in the first half.

"The first half, the Rams were handling us, and maybe our guys had been there a little too long," Sherman said. "Finally out of desperation, Greasy sent . . . me in and two or three of the other scrubbienies, the guys who played on the second team with me, Jim Castiglia, a fullback, and a few others. . . . It was, I don't know, maybe about eight minutes to go in the second quarter or a little more. Well I took them down for a field goal, might have been two field goals, or one field goal, whatever it was, at least we moved the ball.

"Between halves, Greasy really chewed us out . . . Then he turned to me and the other guys who came in with me and said, 'Sherman, you start, you start Castiglia,' and so on. And I had a pretty good second half. I threw two for touchdowns," Sherman said, "We won the game. We came from behind. I threw one to Larry Cabrelli. . . . and then one to (Jack) Ferrante." It was, Sherman was to recount years later, the most memorable day of his playing career.

"An upset," said an Associated Press account of the game, "occurred right off the reel when the world champion Los Angeles Rams, transferred from Cleveland, succumbed to the Philadelphia Eagles, 25 to 14, in the League's first scheduled game ever played on the West Coast. Al Sherman, lightweight quarterback from VMI, passed for two

Philadelphia touchdowns while his mates Roy Zimmerman and Augie Lio booted three field goals."

A dizzying football season was under way.

*****

When World War II was over, Americans came back, in far greater numbers than they had left, to pro football. One could make something out of the inherent similarity in terminology and mentality between football and warfare–from "bombs" to "blitzes" to "ground attacks"–but that really isn't necessary. After victory over Germany and Japan, Americans rediscovered a world of sports and entertainment that the Great Depression and the great war had distracted them from. Football naturally benefited. Now it was up to pro football to keep the interest of those who came to the game. Fortunately for the sport, 1946 was one of the most fascinating years it would ever have.

Right off the bat, Elmer Layden resigned and Bert Bell, co-founder of the Philadelphia Eagles and co-owner of the Pittsburgh Steelers, became the new commissioner of the NFL. In hindsight, Bell has been vilified for a number of different things, on both a personal and pro level. "He wasn't a commissioner, he was a commissar," said former Eagle Frank "Bucko" Kilroy. But there is little doubt that Bell's stewardship from 1946 until his death in 1959 helped the league grow. There were numerous challenges to the league that could have mortally wounded it during those years, and none of them did.

Bell was appointed Jan. 11. A day later, the Cleveland Rams moved to Los Angeles. The importance of this can be overstated: Los Angeles was not the vast television market and metropolis it would become. But it was, even by 1946, one of the nation's biggest cities, and placing a team there was a giant step toward making the NFL truly national in scope. It was a decisive step that major league baseball would not take for another decade, and it paid off for the NFL. The Rams drew an average of 38,700 that first year. It didn't hurt that the team, owned by Dan Reeves, was first-rate. Besides Waterfield, there were such notables as end Jim Benton, running back Tom Harmon, and guard Riley

Matheson to keep interested the fans attracted by the novelty of pro football.

And the Rams were not alone on the West Coast. The 1946 season saw two other teams in California: The Los Angeles Dons and San Francisco 49ers of the new All-America Football Conference. Organized by Arch Ward, sports editor of the Chicago Tribune and father of baseball's all-star game, the AAFC brought football to two other cities that had not had the sport in 1945, Miami and Buffalo, and one that was losing a team, Cleveland.

The league had come together in fits and starts during the war, with would-be owners bailing out before the first game was ever played. The AAFC even made overtures in 1945 to Commissioner Elmer Layden in an attempt to set up a working agreement with the NFL, and the fledgling league was firmly rebuffed. "Let them get a football and play a game and then maybe we'll have something to talk about," was Layden's famous remark. He had no reason to think it would come back to haunt him.

But Ward and company got themselves a football and, in late 1945, they got themselves an NFL owner. Dan Topping's Brooklyn team had merged with the league's Boston franchise for 1945. Now, as part-owner of Yankee Stadium, he wanted to move into Manhattan, something that he claimed the NFL's Giants were not eager to let him do. So, Topping defected to the AAFC, giving the team a solid franchise in the nation's largest city.

There would be other blows struck–the AAFC started signing high-caliber players immediately. Max Morris, an end who broke in with the AAFC's Chicago Rockets in 1946, noted that the war had created a tremendous backlog of players waiting to turn pro or return to pro football in 1946. Several classes of college players had graduated during the war, and while some college players elected to return to campus to use up their eligibility, many others chose to take advantage of the situation and join the pros immediately. By the time that the NFL realized that there really was another league out there, many notable players had been enticed to join the AAFC.

"The Lions, you know, had no reason to worry about me because there was no competition," says Otto Graham, who had been drafted by the NFL's Detroit Lions in 1944. "Later on they found out that I had signed a contract with Paul (Brown) and the Browns, and they wrote and they said, 'Send in a copy of your contract, and we'll see what our lawyer can do about breaking the contract.' And I wrote and said, 'Well, what do you mean break the contract? I signed the contract in good faith. I don't want to break the contract.' That was that simple."

Not every case was as cut-and-dried as Graham made his. The sports pages of the New York Times in 1946 had numerous articles describing cases of contract-jumping, lawsuits, and court rulings. Angelo Bertelli, Paul Governali, Garrard Ramsey, Frank Sinkwich, Chet Adams, and Gaylon Smith were among the players who were the subject of legal and rhetorical tug-of-wars.

Not all such disputes were nasty; the AAFC's Browns allowed star back Ted Fritsch to return to the Green Bay Packers after he had a change of heart about defecting to the new league. And some players left the NFL for the AAFC without looking back. The Eagles, for instance, saw 24-year-old guard Bruno Banducci depart for the San Francisco 49ers, where he would be a fixture until 1954. But the NFL retained most of its notable veterans, including its three top quarterbacks: Sammy Baugh, Sid Luckman, and Bob Waterfield.

The AAFC, however, did quite well with the 1946 rookie class. Some of the men who were to coach AAFC teams in its first year had been affiliated with service teams during the war. Coaching such powerhouses as the Iowa Pre-Flight team or the squad at the Great Lakes Naval Air Station (both of which fielded teams that were on par with the best college teams) gave them extensive insight into the young talent available, as well as personal connections to some of these players. Elroy "Crazy Legs" Hirsch, for instance, recalled he signed with the AAFC's Chicago Rockets because he had played for their coach, Dick Hanley, on the El Toro Marines. No one made better use of his service connections, as well as other non-NFL connections, than Cleveland's Paul Brown.

Brown had made his name coaching in his native Ohio at Massillon High School in the Thirties. Massillon had continued to be a hotbed of football long after pro football left it behind, and in his nine years at Massillon, Brown lost only eight games. Brown took the coaching job at Ohio State in 1941 and won the national championship in 1942. He then took over the highly regarded military team at the Great Lakes Naval Training Station in Illinois. He signed with Cleveland in February 1945 and promptly started rounding up players from his past.

"I, of course," recalled Otto Graham, "had played against Paul Brown's team when he was coaching at Ohio State and I was at Northwestern, and he came down to see me one night. Here he's a lieutenant and, of course, I was a cadet in the Navy Air Corps, and he said, 'We're going to start a new league as soon as the war is over, and Cleveland's going to have a team, and I'm going to be the head coach and general manager,' and he says, 'I want you to be my quarterback.'

"I was making $75 a month as a cadet in the Navy Air Corps," continued Graham, who had finished third in the Heisman Trophy voting in 1943. "And so he said, 'If you will sign the contract with me . . . I will start sending you a check every month as long as the war lasts, for $250.' And he also said, 'I'll give you a $1,000 bonus immediately for signing.' And he said, 'I'll also sign you to a 2-year contract for $7,500 a year.'

"Well, when I thought about making $75 a month, my reaction was, 'Where do I sign?' " laughed Graham. "So I signed the contract with him."

Graham was not the only future star that Brown reeled in. Tackle-kicker Lou Groza, who had played three games of freshmen football at Ohio State in 1942, got a contract from Brown while he was serving on Okinawa. To play end, Brown signed both Dante Lavelli, who had played briefly at Ohio State before entering the Army, and Mac Speedie, whom Brown remembered from the service team at Fort Warren. Except for center Frank Gatski, all of the standouts on the 1946 Browns team were hand-picked by Brown.

Though Brown did bring in some players with pro experience–former Redskins tackle Lou Rymkus was the most notable–many of his players were untested rookies eager to make good. And Brown always told his players that every spot on the roster was up for grabs each and every season.

"Wasn't one car in that training camp," recalled Gatski, who had grown up in West Virginia's coal country, of his experiences that first year. "We all were walk-ons then."

Among the rookies in the two leagues that year were four African-American players. With competition for talent at a premium, it was no longer possible to pretend that black players weren't good enough. The Rams started the ball rolling when, apparently under pressure from the Los Angeles Coliseum Commission, they added Kenny Washington, a longtime local hero. He signed on March 21.

"The first member of his race contracted by a National League Club in 13 years," said the Associated Press account of the signing, "Washington assumed a position in football similar to that of his former teammate at UCLA, Jackie Robinson, Negro infielder signed by the Brooklyn Dodgers for the Montreal farm. . . . Washington, now 27, was rated one of the finest all-around backs ever seen on the coast during his UCLA career, 1937 through 1939."

Signing with the Rams meant that Washington, whose contract was purchased from the minor-league Hollywood Bears of the Pacific Coast Football League, would make it to a major professional league a year before Robinson. He wasn't alone: About six weeks after acquiring Washington, the Rams added end Woody Strode, a 31-year-old black of Indian descent who had played with Washington and Robinson at UCLA. Neither had great success in 1946 for the Rams, with Washington missing much of the season because of recurring knee problems and Strode catching only four passes.

Washington played two more seasons with the Rams. In 1947, he had the league's longest run from scrimmage, 92 yards, and the league's best rushing average, 7.4 yards per carry. Still he was only a shell of the player he had been. "They didn't let him in the football pros until he had a limp," Jim Murray wrote in the Los Angeles Times in 1970. "But he may have been the best ever to play the game . . . He could run like Ernie Nevers, pass like Bob Waterfield, tackle like the Seven Blocks of Granite, and he could block a dog from a pile of fresh meat."

Strode subsequently headed to the Canadian Football League before embarking on a distinguished career as a Hollywood character actor in such action films as *Once Upon a Time in the West, The Man Who Shot Liberty Valance, The Professionals,* and *Sergeant Rutledge.* During the filming of *Spartacus,* Strode recalled, Laurence Olivier approached him and told a deeply humbled Strode that he had been a big fan of him and Washington.

A few months after the signings by the Rams, the AAFC's Cleveland Browns also signed two black players. The first was Bill Willis, a guard who had played for Paul Brown at Ohio State. The circumstances, however, were a bit odd.

Years later, Willis told writer Myron Cope that he waited until August 1946 for an invitation from Brown, but heard nothing. With the season about to begin, Willis prepared to go to Canada to play for the Montreal Alouettes of the Canadian Football League. Shortly before he was to leave, a Columbus sportswriter coaxed a reluctant Willis to go to Bowling Green, Ohio, and more or less ask for a tryout with the Browns.

Whether Brown put that sportswriter up to calling Willis is not known, though it is often assumed that Brown did that so that Willis' appearance would not cause a commotion. Regardless, Brown's "networking" certainly helped Willis once he was there. Willis said that there were so many other former Ohio State players in camp that his presence caused no real fuss. He soon played his way into the lineup.

Willis was subsequently joined by Marion Motley, a fullback and linebacker from the University of Nevada. There is considerable dispute about the facts concerning Motley's signing. Motley, at times, expressed some bitterness toward the Browns and suggested that he was only brought in because Bill Willis had already won a spot on the team and needed someone to room with. These things are known: 1) Brown knew Motley from his days at McKinley High School in Canton and had coached him at Great Lakes, 2) Motley did not join the Browns until fellow fullback Ted Fritsch had returned to the Packers, and 3) Motley did end up rooming with Willis.

But even if one believes that Brown brought in Motley to be the "roommate," it is clear that Brown realized what a talented player he was getting. When Motley joined the Browns, he had another year of eligibility at Nevada remaining. In order to compensate the school for its loss, Paul Brown sent a player to Jim Aiken, Nevada's coach and an old friend of Brown's from his high school days in Ohio.

Paul Brown "wanted Motley for his team; he felt that he would complement the rest of his squad," said Bill Mackrides, who was then a quarterback at Nevada. "He made an agreement, that if they (the University of Nevada) would let him have Motley–of course, he could have signed Motley, but he was a gentlemen about it–he would send him a football player for a year to take his place." In 1993, Michael Connors of Nevada's Sports Information Office told me that former Athletics Director Dick Trachok confirmed Mackrides' story as being basically true.

Brown's gift to Nevada was end Horace Gillom, who had been a star for Brown at Massillon. Gillom played the 1946 season at Nevada and then in 1947 joined the Browns, for whom he was an outstanding punter for many years. (Gillom was the team's third black player, arriving in Cleveland the same year that Cleveland Indians owner Bill Veeck integrated baseball's American League by signing Larry Doby.)

The signing of Willis and Motley gave Brown six future Hall-of-Famers in his 1946 rookie class. Not surprisingly, Cleveland ended up winning the AAFC's first championship easily. Except for consecutive midseason losses to the 49ers and Dons, the Browns were devastating, posting wins by such scores as 44-0, 51-14, 66-14, and 42-17. They ended the regular season with a 34-0 victory over Miami in Florida, a game in which Motley and Willis were not able to play because Florida prohibited integrated sporting events. For the season, the Browns established a mark for pro football by averaging more than 57,000 fans per game.

In the championship game Dec. 22, the New York Yankees gave the Browns a fierce fight, but Cleveland prevailed, 14-9, on the strength of a fourth-quarter touchdown pass from Otto Graham to Dante Lavelli. Graham then sealed the win by intercepting an Ace Parker pass.

Marion Motley scored the other Cleveland touchdown. He rushed for 98 yards on 13 carries, outgaining the Yankees' Spec Sanders, who had led the AAFC in rushing, while Graham outdueled the veteran Parker, completing 16 passes for 213 yards. Graham, Motley, Willis and Lavelli were named All-AAFC.

The NFL title game was an even more eventful one. During the season, the league had shattered all its attendance records, helped by the fact that eight of the 10 teams posted non-losing records. The league's best mark was posted by the Chicago Bears. With a deep backfield featuring Sid Luckman, Hugh Gallerneau, George McAfee, Dante Magnani, and Bill Osmanski, and such standout linemen as Bulldog Turner, Fred Davis, Chuck Drulis, and Ray Bray, the Bears went 8-2-1 and held off the Rams, Packers, and Cardinals in the West.

In the East, the Redskins started fast but collapsed after Oct. 27, when they blew a 24-0 lead to the Eagles and lost, 28-24. The Eagles beat the Giants the following week to move into serious contention, but then lost to the Giants, Pittsburgh, and Washington to see their title chances go down the drain. After beating the Eagles, the Giants derailed the surprising Steelers and closed the season with a 31-0 victory over Washington to win the East and set up a title game Dec. 15 with the Bears.

"Steve Owen's teams are always tough to move on, but this one is exceptional," Bears coach George Halas told the Associated Press three days before the game. "Last Sunday, the Giants not only outcharged the powerful Washington line, but rushed Sammy Baugh so consistently he simply didn't have time to locate his receivers and get his passes away." Halas' Bears, nevertheless, were favored by 10 points.

On the day of the championship game, a scandal broke. There came word that a convicted felon named Sidney Paris had been arrested, charged with trying to bribe Giants quarterback Frank Filchock and fullback Merle Hapes to lose the game. The night before, the two players had been summoned to the home of New York City's mayor and confronted with allegations of the fix attempt. Hapes admitted the bribe attempt and was suspended by commissioner Bert Bell; Filchock denied any knowledge of it and was allowed to play.

With that onus on their shoulders, the Giants played the Bears as if everybody's integrity were at stake. All accounts of the game describe Filchock as playing furiously, even though he broke his nose in the first quarter. "To use an old expression, Filchock played like a man possessed," recalled Jim Keane, who was a rookie end for the Bears that season.

Filchock wasn't particularly impressive, throwing six interceptions, one of which was returned by Dante Magnani for a first-quarter touchdown that gave the Bears a 14-0 lead. Filchock did, however, lead the Giants storming back from that early deficit, throwing touchdown passes to Frank Liebel and Steve Filopowicz to tie the game. That tie held until the fourth quarter when Chicago's Sid Luckman, a quarterback not known for his running, faked to George McAfee and ran 19 yards for the winning score. The Bears won, 24-14.

Unlike earlier scandals, this one did not seem to do serious damage to the league. "The large noise left over today from the National Football League 1946 World Series wasn't so much about the return of the Chicago Bears to the top spot as it was the fight the New York Giants put up before the big and bruising Bears were able to turn the trick," began an Associated Press account of the game.

"They didn't win but then they didn't figure to against the might of the Monsters (of the Midway, Chicago's nickname), and their quarterback genius Sid Luckman, who tossed for one touchdown, scored another on a 'cute' 19-yard trick sprint that caught the Giants' flat-footed, and who equaled or bettered four playoff records for passing and grabbing interceptions," the account continued.

Hapes and Filchock were each barred from the league for a number of years for failing to report the bribe, but the NFL was not seriously wounded. The principal image that came out of this game was not one of seedy characters, but of players fighting tooth and nail against what was probably a better team to prove their integrity. Commissioner Bert Bell got points for damage control as well. The subsequent trials for the gamblers involved in the fix attempt did not paint the players in the best possible light; they had been, after all, hanging around, with undesirable types and there were stories of womanizing and drinking. But it was soon evident that the league had managed to avert disaster.

What was not evident at the time was that this title game was a last hurrah of sorts for the four teams that had dominated league play for many years: The Bears, Giants, Redskins, and Packers. None of these teams would return to a championship game until 1956, and other than the Giants, none of them would win another title until the Sixties.

The Bears remained strong for the rest of the Forties, but fell just short each year. They began to struggle in the Fifties, and since then it has been the exception, rather than the rule, for them to be title contenders. After winning five of the league's first 14 titles, they have won only two since 1946. Hurt by the loss of Filchock, the Giants had three rough seasons before bouncing back into contention in 1950, while the Packers and Redskins did not re-emerge as contenders for many years.

The 1946 also featured the last of another NFL tradition: the all-around star who was so great that he seemed to be playing every position on the field. In 1946, that player was Bill Dudley, and in the worthy tradition of Jim Thorpe, Bronko Nagurski and Ernie Nevers, "The Bluefield Bullet" was a dominant force for the Pittsburgh Steelers.

Unlike those three, whose legends are built primarily on myth, Dudley had a mountain of statistics to support his value. He led the NFL in seven categories in 1946: Rushing yardage, rushing attempts, interceptions, yardage on interceptions, punt returns, punt return yardage, and average gain on punt returns. He was also Pittsburgh's primary punter, passer, place-kicker and kick returner, as well as its leading scorer. Dudley was named the league's most valuable player.

All of this came during a season in which Dudley was having serious difficulties with his coach, Jock Sutherland; their relationship was so strained that Dudley never played for the Steelers again. Still, nobody has achieved anything like what Dudley did in 1946 in all of the football seasons since. Gushed writer Robert Leckie: "Bill Dudley, like Jim Thorpe and Bronko Nagurski and Ernie Nevers, specialized in everything."

*****

After their auspicious beginning in Los Angeles, the Eagles won five more games in 1946 to end up in second place in the NFL's Eastern

Division for the third straight year. The team had mixed success in signing players: They lost 1945 first-round pick John Yonakor to Cleveland, but did sign fullback-linebacker Joe Muha of VMI, their 1943 first-round choice. Besides Muha, their rookie class included several other players who would play key roles in the next few years, including back Russ Craft of Alabama, guard-kicker Cliff Patton of Texas Christian, and tackle Jay MacDowell of Washington. They lost veteran guard Bruno Banducci to the AAFC, but traded for Augie Lio, a guard who also handled the team's kicking chores, and Alex Wojciechowicz, a player who had long been regarded as one of the NFL's best centers.

But the single most important triumph for the franchise that year may have come in April. That was when they signed back Steve Van Buren to a three-year contract, ending any possibility that he would jump to the AAFC. Unlike fellow back Bill Dudley, Van Buren was not a passer or a kicker or a key defender. But he was a great running back, and running backs such as Van Buren–coupled with the T formation offense brought to the NFL by George Halas and refined by coaches like Greasy Neale–would soon make all-purpose tailbacks like Bill Dudley scarce.

The predominant offense in the NFL for many years had been the single wing. That offense utilized seven players on the line, including two ends, either of whom could catch passes. There were four players in the backfield, any of whom could theoretically receive the center's snap and then pass or hand off or run with the ball. Plays took a long time in forming because blockers had to move themselves into position after the ball was snapped.

With the single wing, each member of the backfield had to be versatile enough to run or pass the ball when called upon to do so. That's not to say that coaches did not use players according to their best skills; Slingin' Sammy Baugh did most of the passing for the Redskins. But the single wing, at its best, required several backs who were good at everything, and those players are never easy to come by.

The T formation was brought to pro football by George Halas. The offense, so named because of the "T" that the four backs make in lining up, had been employed as far back as the 1880s, but it had been largely abandoned at the expense of other strategies in the Twenties. The Bears started using the T formation in the early Thirties, but it wasn't until the late 1930s that Halas, with the help of college coach Clark Shaughnessy, made it different. The T as used by the Bears was an offense based on movement and deception. Halas told writer Allison Danzig that as many of nine of 11 players on the field might be in motion before the snap of the ball.

"Primarily," Halas told Danzig, "we do not look upon the T as an attacking formation. Instead, we consider the T as a convenient way of lining up our players so that they can shift speedily into whichever attacking formation seems best calculated to overcome the opponents' type of defense."

Not only did they use man-in-motion plays but also plays designed to send the ballcarrier in the direction opposite from where the man-in-motion went. In 1940, the Bears added plays in which they split one of the ends out wide (a wide receiver) and sent a man-in-motion to the opposite side.

The Halas offense must have looked like a fire drill, with players shifting and spinning in every direction almost every play. The idea was, in the famous words of baseball great Wee Willie Keeler, to "hit 'em where they ain't" by quickly finding a breach in the defense and getting a ballcarrier through it. The Bears' T also made more extensive use of the passing game than other pro offenses had; for one thing, the formation made it possible to create a pocket of blockers in the backfield from which the quarterback could survey the field and throw from. Moreover, their quarterback was a specialist. Sid Luckman, a Columbia star who entered the NFL in 1939, did not have to worry about running or blocking; those duties fell to the other three backs in the lineup. Luckman's main job was to pass, and few have ever done it better.

"The T," wrote University of Missouri Coach Don Faurot in 1950, "has all the ingredients of customer satisfaction. It has definite high-scoring possibilities. It stresses excellent deceptiveness and speed, rather than power. It makes frequent use of laterals and forward passes, always the 'thrill plays.' "

Anyone who doubted its effectiveness had only to look to the 1940

NFL title game, where the Bears beat the Redskins by the astounding score of 73-0. The Bears found holes in Washington's defense and then ran wild: There were touchdowns of 68, 42, 30, and 44 yards. Late in the game, referee Red Friesel asked the Bears to either pass or run for their extra points instead of kicking them. So many footballs had already been booted into the stands that they were running out of them.

Wrote Stanley Woodward of The New York Herald Tribune after the game: "The great Halas has been fooling around with the T formation for years, but he has never given such a vivid demonstration of the virulence which may be forthcoming from it as he did today." The 73-point margin of victory remains the biggest in NFL history. Three years later, Luckman threw for seven touchdowns in one game against the Giants, setting another record that remains unsurpassed.

"The resurgence of pro football is with that T formation and getting out of the other game," recalled Eagles lineman Frank "Bucko" Kilroy, who became a pro in 1943. "I played the other game; I liked it, but I mean it wasn't a spectator's game . . . When they all went to the T formation, it became a great spectator game."

Still, it took years for everybody in pro football to adopt the T. For one thing, the science of scouting was different than it is today. It was not as if a coach could just watch game films of the Bears, study them, and diagram plays for his team accordingly. With the use of game films being limited, information about your foes–and their strategies–was hard to come by.

In 1941, according to writer Tom Bennett, new Philadelphia coach Greasy Neale purchased film of the Bears' 73-0 victory from Fox Movietone News for $156 and began converting the Eagles to a T offense. Back Jack Hinkle recalled Neale also "got some ideas from different players that had played some T." One of those players apparently was center Frank Bausch, who played four seasons with the Bears before joining the Eagles in 1941.

Neale added some original concepts. Unlike Halas, who relied primarily on his fullback (the man who lined up at the center point of the "T") to run the ball, Neale would use the fullback to block and the halfbacks to run. There were some fakes designed to pull defenders away from the spot where the ballcarrier was headed, but Neale was also interested in the formation as a way to blow through the opponents' line. His T formation was intended to create a power running game.

"Now the Bears' T was a different T than ours," recalled Frank "Bucko" Kilroy. "Theirs was by deception, trickery, and all that. And ours was a T, the first of what they call Winged T. It was power."

This, after all, was in an era when many coaches thought of the forward pass as a risky venture; Eagles tackle Al Wistert, who coached high school football in his spare time, recounted that Neale taught him not to throw the ball any farther than the game situation warranted. Your passing attack was not your primary weapon–though it had better be good, just in case.

"Greasy Neale's attitude was," recounted end Dick Humbert, "we're going to have an offensive team that can run the ball first, pass the ball second, but our passing attack had to be near as good as anybody else's. That way, if they tried to load up and stop our football running attack, we'd throw."

Now that he had an offensive strategy, Neale needed the players to carry it out. To get a quarterback for the 1941 season, Neale traded end Don Looney to Pittsburgh for Tommy Thompson.

To say Thompson was an unlikely field general is an understatement. At the age of 12 in Fort Worth, Texas, Thompson had been blinded in his left eye by a stone thrown by another child. This injury deprived Thompson of depth perception and made him susceptible to being slammed to the ground by defenders that he never saw.

No one seemed to know how old Thompson was. It was known that he had played college ball, first at Alabama, then at Tulsa, in the late Thirties (he was named All-Missouri Valley Conference in 1938), but it's not clear how old he was when he got to those schools. A 1949 article in an Eagles game program even made light of "Tommyhawk Tommy" and his fluctuating age, which by this time had gone in the NFL guide from 29 in 1946 to 30 in 1947 to 29 in 1948 and 30 in 1949. "Thompson," wrote Frank O'Gara, "as cagey about the total of his summers as an old maid, currently admits to 29–and hotly disputes the suggestion that he has lopped off a twelve month here and there."

But Thompson couldn't stand to lose at anything, and it was this attitude that made Greasy Neale and Thompson perfectly suited not only to lead this ballclub, but also to become close friends and buddies on the golf course.

"Tommy was good at about everything that he tried, I assume. He was a good card player. He was a good gambler, on the golf course and with a deck of cards in his hands. He was an excellent golfer," recalled Jim Parmer, a back who joined the Eagles in 1948. "In Hibbing, Minnesota, one time when we were training up in Minnesota . . . (golfing great) Byron Nelson came up and played with; Byron and Tommy played against two of the local pros, and Tommy outscored Byron Nelson."

Parmer also recalled that Thompson and his wife, Dodie, herself an excellent golfer, would go to Florida in the offseason with $1500 and after a few months of playing golf, come back with three times that amount.

On the football field, Thompson was an outstanding passer, but his old teammates remember him most of all as a great leader, comparable to latter-day heroes John Elway and Roger Staubach in the way that he thrived on pressure and cherished the role of field general.

"He had so much bravery. He had so much heart," tackle Al Wistert said at the time of Thompson's death. "When someone knocked him down, he'd get right back up and throw a strike."

Vic Lindskog, Thompson's longtime center, recalled, "When he said something in the huddle, everybody, well that's it. In other words, he'd cuss your ass out if you didn't listen to him and do what he said."

Parmer recalled, "Tommy had an excellent football mind. He was a calculating football player. He could piss ice water, or certainly gave you that impression whether he felt that way or not. I've been in the bunk above him on sleeper trains going from coast to coast, and . . . I'd hear him wrestling around, smoking cigarettes. He slept very little the night before a ballgame. It may have all been a facade, but to me and all the rest of us, Tommy was a helluva football player, a great leader, and a winner."

Added Parmer, "Tommy was the leader of our football team. Nobody else. That Tommy Thompson was."

Thompson took over at quarterback in 1941 and played two years before heading off to the service. (Despite his disability, he served in Europe.) When he returned, he was able to win back his job from the two men who had been playing the position in his absence, Allie Sherman and Roy Zimmerman. Sherman, who had come to the Eagles out of VMI at the age of 20 in 1943, stayed through 1947. He spent most of that time as a backup, before beginning a long and distinguished coaching career. Zimmerman had made the UPI All-Pro team for his performance at quarterback in 1944, but lost the Eagles' job to Thompson in 1946 and ended up with the Detroit Lions in 1947. "Zimmerman had a pretty good arm, but he didn't have the touch that this other guy had," recalled tackle Frank "Bucko" Kilroy, who added that Zimmerman "wasn't the type to grab the bull by the horns."

If anyone had any doubts that Thompson had the talent and fire to lead the Eagles, those would have been eliminated after their game Oct. 27, 1946 in Washington.

The Redskins jumped out to a 24-0 halftime lead, but Thompson led the team back in the second half. After a touchdown by Ernie Steele, Thompson threw touchdown passes to Bosh Pritchard and Gil Steinke to close within three points. With less than two minutes to play, Thompson hit Jack Ferrante for a 30-yard touchdown pass to give the Eagles a 28-24 victory. At the time, it was the biggest come-from-behind victory in league history.

By 1946, Neale had also found a top-flight ballcarrier. In the early years, he had relied primarily on Jack Hinkle, Ernie Steele, and a gregarious waiver-wire acquisition named Bosh Pritchard. All of them were good enough to make significant contributions to winning teams for several years, but none of them was a superstar. In 1944, Neale found his stud horse: a 23-year-old rookie from Louisiana State University named Steve Van Buren.

Van Buren was born in Honduras on Dec. 28, 1920, son of an

American fruit inspector and his Spanish wife. A few years later, he and his younger brother Ebert were orphaned, and they came to New Orleans to live with their grandparents. At first too small to play football, Steve dropped out of high school to work in an iron foundry.

When he returned to Warren Easton High School, he tried the game again. "I went out for running back in high school. They put me at end," Van Buren recalled. "I got a scholarship to LSU at end." At LSU, he studied mechanical engineering, ran track, and became a blocking back.

"I only ran the ball my last year," he recalled. "Before, I was blocking back and linebacker, but I always wanted to run the ball. In fact, the old coach saw me a few years later and said, 'Steve, I did you a terrible injustice.' "

As a senior in 1943, Van Buren led the nation in scoring and led LSU to an Orange Bowl triumph, a victory that Van Buren said he savored more than any other. Apparently on the recommendation of LSU's coach, the Eagles drafted Van Buren in the first round in 1944. At that time, Van Buren had never heard of the Eagles and when he took the train to Philadelphia, he missed his stop and ended up in New York City. When he finally showed up at the team's training camp, he hardly looked the role of a star. Neale, the story goes, took one look at Van Buren–carrying a battered suitcase and wearing shoes but no socks–and told back Allie Sherman to get him some clothes.

"I went to the (annual College) All-Star Game and I had my appendix out," Van Buren said of his arrival with the Eagles. "When I first went to the Eagles, it was still bleeding a little bit, you know, and I wore a corset. The coach couldn't understand why my leg didn't seem too strong."

Nevertheless, it didn't take Van Buren long to establish himself; he was All-Pro in 1944 and 1945. It took him longer, however, to adjust to being a star. Unlike his longtime backfield mate Bosh Pritchard, who could be counted on to find any piano or microphone that was available when the team was out in public, Van Buren seemed out of place in the limelight.

"I can remember one incident," said fellow back Jim Parmer, "that a car dealer, a Ford car dealer, told Steve that if he would endorse a Ford, he would give him a Ford convertible to drive. Steve said, 'No thanks, I drive a Cadillac' and turned him down cold, and didn't take the car.

"I," laughed Parmer, "and probably all 37 or whatever we had, would have jumped at that opportunity, but Steve turned it down."

Though he was close to Alex Wojciechowicz, Van Buren's teammates found him hard to get to know and a bit unusual. Parmer said Van Buren never washed a shirt–he just discarded the one he was wearing and bought a new one whenever appropriate. Van Buren was also a notoriously bad driver; he told writer Myron Cope of one day when he wrecked three cars. "I was going only 5 miles an hour when I got hit by some of them, you know, I never got in an accident for going too *fast,*" he said.

Van Buren did like fast horses: He, Wojciechowicz, Thompson, and Greasy Neale were all fond of betting on horse racing. He was also humble (a 1949 Eagles program described him as "prone to underestimate own ability"), easygoing, and well-liked.

"He was a good man," Parmer said of Van Buren. "Always had a smile for a rookie, which a lot of them didn't. You didn't get close to him–or I certainly didn't–but I think I could call him a friend. Steve was a quiet man, didn't have a whole lot to say, really, to anybody. He more or less did his talking on the ballfield. But if you struck up a conversation with him–you kinda had to drag it out of him–he'd certainly sit there and talk to you."

On the field, Van Buren was blind fury. His running style was simple: He took the ball in his right hand, put his head down, headed up the middle, and burrowed through anything in front of him. "Steve struck fear into the heart of a defense. When he hit the line, he looked like a bulldozer going through a picket fence," fellow back Russ Craft told writer Phil Anastasia.

He was, in the words of Vic Lindskog, a "skimmer," running low to the ground for balance. And though he was known as a power runner, he was also fast.

"Van Buren never runs to the sidelines if an extra yard is to be gained by going straight ahead," wrote Ed Hogan in a 1949 Eagles game program. "He is entirely unmindful of himself, physically, and almost contemptuous of anything in front of him. Over, under, or around he goes–and preferably over."

When somebody got him mad, he turned himself into a battering ram. A number of his former teammates told stories of opposing players taunting or poking or gouging Van Buren until he got to the point where he called for the ball–and told everyone else to get out of the way. Those stories, true or not, generally ended with Van Buren trampling his tormentor.

"Boy, he left guys kicking," Al Wistert said. "He was a great runner. A great, great, great runner."

One of Van Buren's most famous runs occurred against the Detroit Lions in an exhibition game Sept. 19, 1946. Playing with a fever, Van Buren scored on a 65-yard run in which he zigged and zagged across the field. This is a description from the book *Great Pro Running Backs*: "Practically every Lion had a shot at him, and five times he was knocked down. But, as the rules permitted in that era, he quickly scrambled back to his feet each time and kept going until he reached the end zone."

Though he was an exceptional kick returner and was regarded as a more-than-adequate defender his first few years in the league, he was not as versatile as Bill Dudley. For one thing, he didn't throw the ball and didn't like to have it thrown to him. "The guy who threw the first forward pass," Van Buren was known to say, "must have been through as a football player or just too tired that day to run with the ball." Bill Mackrides, a quarterback who joined the Eagles in 1947, recalled Van Buren telling him in the huddle: "Hand it to me, don't throw it to me."

Fortunately, the T formation employed by Greasy Neale did not require Van Buren to do much other than run with the ball. This made Van Buren the prototype for the "franchise" running back that just about every team would deem essential in years to come, a war horse whom teams could ride up and down the field. In 1945, he scored 18 touchdowns in 10 games, setting an NFL record that stood until Green Bay's Jim Taylor, playing a 14-game schedule, scored 19 touchdowns in 1962. (Of the great runners of latter years, Taylor and Earl Campbell of the Houston Oilers were probably the closest to Van Buren in terms of running style.)

"He made me a great coach," Greasy Neale was often quoted as saying about Van Buren. "He was better than (Red) Grange because Grange needed a blocker. This boy didn't. He could run away from tacklers like Red, or over them like (Bronko) Nagurski."

In 1946, Neale had Thompson and Van Buren together in his T formation offense for the first time. But Van Buren was plagued by injuries, and his production fell from 110 points to 36. Bosh Pritchard, Gil Steinke, and Jack Ferrante took up some of the offensive slack, but the team still scored fewer points than it had in 1945. More important, the offense was barely able to outscore the defense, 231-220. Clearly, Neale had done a better job designing his offense than his defense. So, Neale, always the tinkerer, went to work.

In the early years of pro football, defensive strategy was rather limited. In the Twenties, seven, eight, or nine players played on the line of scrimmage; players who lined up behind the line of scrimmage were basically safety valves in case the resistance at the point of the attack collapsed. Linemen played in the same place that they did on offense (though the ends might be split a little wider on defense than on offense), so the same players were hitting each other on both sides of the ball.

And hit each other was what they did: One was not taught to diagnose plays, but merely to push the player who was pushing you, knock down the player who was trying to knock you down. Defensive strategy was not very imaginative: Most coaches worried about offense first and let the defense largely take care of itself.

As the sport evolved, new defensive plays and formations came about primarily when it had become apparent that the old defenses simply didn't work. That was the case in the Thirties when NFL teams created defensive formations with three layers of players, placing more men back from the line of scrimmage. This tactic was designed to give each team a second line of resistance composed of three "linebackers." Behind the linebackers, as many as three other players were stationed as a backfield to handle pass plays and runners who broke into the clear. Pulling men back from the line of scrimmage increased the mobility of the defense.

By the mid-Forties, it was apparent that the T formation had overwhelmed these defenses too. The biggest problem was that as many as four offensive players (the two ends and two halfbacks) were apt to go downfield for a pass, and there were only three men in the defensive backfield to cover them. That meant that linebackers were left to chase down some fast players. With motion offenses in vogue, this could be particularly worrisome–somebody was apt to get free and catch the ball before anyone noticed where he was. A change was necessary.

The solution that Greasy Neale came up with was to add another player to the defensive backfield, improving his team's ability to cover pass plays. In the process, the middle of the three linebackers would be eliminated but the two linebackers that remained would be more important than ever. It would be their jobs to smother the passing game at the line of scrimmage by flattening the ends–a tactic that was legal then. The formation would be a 5-2-4 alignment; it would have five linemen (including a middle guard who had to hold the center of the line together), two linebackers, and four men in the secondary.

By the end of the 1946 season, Neale was ready to test this defense, and his guinea pig–the man who was to move off the line and become the fourth man in the defensive backfield–was Dick Humbert. Known as "Banana Hands" because of his huge hands, Humbert was an end from the University of Richmond then in his third year with the Eagles. He recounted that Neale came to him late in the 1946 season and asked, "Wouldn't it be easier for you to cover a man if you were a little off the line of scrimmage, and to the off-side?" Humbert said he thought it would.

Neale and Humbert worked on this concept in practice, though they never mentioned it to anyone else. Humbert recalled that he told Neale that he thought it would work not only for pass defense, but also for run defense because he realized he was getting "a better view of the run, being off in the back a little bit." Before the final game of 1946, it was agreed that Neale would signal Humbert at some point in the game, at which time he would drop back into the secondary.

"So, it was either right after the half started or right before the half–it may have been after the half because he didn't want to give them a chance to check on it at halftime–anyhow, he gave me the nod to go ahead and drop off," Humbert said. "I dropped back out off-side about three yards or so, back about two or three yards, just backed right off the line of scrimmage. And, the quarterback looked up and saw me over there. Boy, right away, he poured a sweep that way and, of course, I thought it was very easy to come up from there, because you could see it so easy . . . . You could see everything. I went right up in there and stopped the play.

"So, next play, he came back out and I backed out again. He decided well, he'd throw in there behind me. Well, I was in a perfect position to be able to get back and help the halfback out on the flat pass over there."

After a few more plays, Neale signaled Humbert that he had seen enough. The Eagles won the game, 40-14, clinching second place behind the Giants. The Associated Press account noted that an "infuriated" Eagles line had thoroughly shut down Boston's rushing attack. It's doubtful, however, that very many people took notice of the new defense that Neale had briefly employed.

In the offseason, Neale continued to work on his defense. Before the 1947 season, the Eagles, with Dick Humbert now playing defensive back, practiced the new 5-2-4 defense but played their old defense in exhibition games so as not to tip off their opponents. When the season started, Neale unveiled his defense. The 5-2-4 soon became known as the "Eagle Defense," and it changed the way that defense was played in pro football.

3

1947—THE MEN IN UNIFORM

****

The 1947 rookie class was weaker than the enormous and gifted Class of 1946. Many players whose classes had graduated during the war had taken advantage of the NFL-AAFC bidding war to turn pro in 1946, while others had gone back to college to get their degrees. Not many players had enrolled in college during the war, so the actual Class of 1947 was not a big one. And some first-rate athletes still passed up the lure of pro football. The Redskins, for instance, used their first pick in 1946 on Cal Rossi, only to discover that the UCLA halfback was not eligible to turn pro. In 1947, they again used their first-round pick on him, only to discover that he wasn't interested.

The best prospects available in 1947 were mostly players who could have come out in 1946, but who chose to go back to college for another year. The most heralded of these was Charley Trippi, once dubbed "the greatest thing to come out of the South since the invention of the cotton gin." The University of Georgia all-American, nicknamed "Golden Boy," was sought not only by the two football leagues, but also by baseball's New York Yankees. He chose to sign with the NFL's Chicago Cardinals. Shortly after Trippi turned pro, Jim Thorpe, the legend by which all other football legends were measured, called Trippi "the greatest football player I ever saw."

Being as that only one team could land Trippi, other teams had to find their talent elsewhere. Rebuffed by Cal Rossi, the Redskins did add one notable rookie in 1947, Hugh "Bones" Taylor of Oklahoma City University. He had been signed by Washington after Coach Turk Edwards read about him in a magazine. On Sept. 28, 1947, in his first game as a pro, Taylor was spectacular, catching touchdown passes of 62, 36, and 18 yards from Sammy Baugh against the Eagles. Overall, Taylor had eight receptions for 212 yards against Greasy Neale's newly unveiled defense.

The Eagles had a pair of rookie ends of their own. In 1946, Tommy Thompson's primary receiver had been former minor-league star Jack Ferrante, but when the 1947 season opened, Thompson had been given two new weapons. One of his new targets was gentlemanly Neill Armstrong of Oklahoma A&M, the team's first-round draft choice. On his first play in the NFL, Armstrong caught a touchdown pass from Thompson.

The Eagles also had added rugged Pete "The Golden Greek" Pihos from the University of Indiana. Only slightly less heralded than Trippi, the 23-year-old Pihos had finally signed with the team two years after they drafted him. Against Washington, he showed that he was worth the wait by catching five passes, two of them for touchdowns.

The rookie ends were not the only stars that day. Baugh, poised to embark on what was to be his greatest season, threw for a total of five touchdowns, and Eddie Saenz returned a kickoff 94 yards. The Eagles, meanwhile, got a 95-yard kick return by Steve Van Buren and a short touchdown run by Allie Sherman in pulling out a 45-42 victory. The Associated Press described it simply as a "super-duper thriller." It was, at the time, the highest-scoring NFL game ever.

*****

There were not many hard-and-fast rules about locating football players in the Forties. In some ways, World War II changed them all, and in some ways it did not change any of them.

It's clear that there were any number of roads that a player could take to the NFL and AAFC at the time. During this era the only real constant, the only thing that just about all pro football players had in common, was that their lives were dramatically interrupted by World War II.

The Sports Encyclopedia: Pro Football lists hundreds of players as having served in World War II and that list only includes those who left pro football to go off to war. Hundreds more, like Pete Pihos, turned pro after the war was over. Others were stationed stateside or served in defense-related jobs. Many of those who went overseas saw extensive combat; many were decorated for bravery. Eighteen current or former pro football players were killed in action.

Much has been written about the effect the war had on these players, how it gave them a certain focus that they might have lacked otherwise. Steelers guard Nick Skorich told writer Stuart Leuthner, "I think we came back from the war more mature, with a little more perspective, and knew the direction we wanted to go." Also in Leuthner's book, Frank "Bucko" Kilroy is quoted as saying that the first question asked about a player in those days was not what school had he gone to, but what outfit had he served in. Whatever the real effect, it's undoubtedly true that the war defined this generation of players.

"I really believe that our ideas and attitudes were shaped by the three-to four-year interruption of our lives, caused by WWII," recalled Eagles back Russ Craft. "After what many of us had been through, it was great and true happiness to get back home and get our lives on track doing what most of us loved most."

Or as Browns end Dante Lavelli told writer Terry Pluto: "Just coming home in one piece and being able to play football–that was an honor."

Service to their country aside, the professional football players of this era had widely divergent backgrounds. The colleges were a steady source of talent, but pro coaches rarely saw many college players in person, so they had to rely on recommendations and guesswork to find the best of them. There were, of course, those players who theoretically were "can't miss" talents (presuming that they would chose to turn pro). These were the golden boys of college football: Charley Trippi was one; Pete Pihos was another. They made drafting easy.

But no team was fortunate enough to be able to fill a roster with blue-chip players, so teams had to find other sources for players. And since teams spend very little money on scouting, these players often came to them. They came from colleges, big and small. Sometimes they came recommended; sometimes, like in the case of Washington's Bones Taylor, someone had read or heard something about the athlete and figured he was worth a gamble. Sometimes, too, they came from places other than colleges. There were military teams and minor league teams–both could be sources of players. And sometimes the players came, as Philadelphia's Jack Ferrante did, from the sandlots. The trick for any franchise was in finding the right mix of each type of player, as the Eagles did when they teamed up Pihos and Ferrante at end.

Few players personified the collegiate golden boy better than Pete Pihos. This Army veteran was the kind of player who left college coaches and sportswriters gasping for adjectives.

Pihos came to Indiana University from Chicago's Austin High School in 1942. He had played his first two years of high school ball in Orlando, Fla., before moving to Chicago, where he was an all-city end for two years. After hearing coach Bo McMillin speak at a banquet, he opted to go to Indiana.

At that time, Midwestern football, particularly that of the Big Ten (which was then also called the Western Conference), was probably as good as it has ever been. A Big Ten school, Minnesota, won the national championship in 1940 and 1941, followed by Ohio State in 1942 and a Midwestern independent, Notre Dame, in 1943 Among the other Big Ten schools, Michigan, Northwestern, Wisconsin, and Purdue all made the Top 10 in those years. The pros were loaded with their alumni; from 1937 to 1944, Green Bay used eight straight first-round draft choices on players from the conference.

With its pageantry, enthusiasm and majesty, Big Ten football was perceived as being a purer and grander version of the game than the one played in the NFL. This was a league of student-athletes, one whose athletes were expected to take academics seriously and be good citizens. Pihos majored in business administration at Indiana and later spent more than two years in law school, though he never became a lawyer. At Indiana, he met and married Dorothy Lansing, who was on her way to becoming a doctor.

Pete Pihos played his first two seasons with the Hoosiers at end, garnering some all-American honors in his sophomore year. "He's the best pass receiver of the year," raved noted writer Grantland Rice, who selected him to his 1943 all-American team in Colliers magazine.

Then Pihos went to war, serving in the Army's 35th Infantry. He went in a private and came back from Europe a second lieutenant with five battle stars, having seen significant action in the Battle of the Bulge. In 1945, he returned to Indiana, where Bo McMillin shifted the rock-solid 205-pounder to fullback and told him to call the plays.

The 1945 Hoosiers team was loaded: Back George Taliaferro would be good enough to play seven seasons in the NFL, center John Cannady would play eight years for the Giants, and others would also make it to the pros. End Ted Kluzewski chose baseball over pro football, becoming one of baseball's top sluggers during the Fifties. But it was Pihos who is best-remembered from that squad. Coming out of the service, he joined the team after it had pulled off an opening-week upset of Michigan. Arriving on a Tuesday, he played 56 minutes against Northwestern on the following Saturday. In the final minutes of the game, he bulled his way through an army of tacklers to score the touchdown that tied the game at 7.

The game ended at that score and Indiana went on to win the conference with a 9-0-1 record. The team climbed all the way to fourth in the Associated Press polls; the Hoosiers have never finished a season ranked higher than that. Pihos ended up as a second-team all-American, finishing behind Army legend Doc Blanchard in the voting.

"Pete is the most complete football player I've ever coached," McMillin said. "Pete could play any position on the team better than the person we had playing it–in fact, in most cases better than anyone else in the country." A caption in *The History of American Football,* published in 1956, says Pihos "can be classed as one of the truly remarkable football players of modern times. He was a first-rate tackle and a powerful fullback at Indiana." Years later, Pihos would be named the best player in Indiana history.

Neither Pihos nor the Hoosiers had as good a season in 1946, but Pihos was still a hot property. The Eagles, who had drafted him in 1945, signed him for the 1947 season. It was a coup for the team, which had a poor record when it came to signing the players it drafted.

When he arrived, Pihos was brash. Vic Sears, by then an All-Pro tackle, remembered that Greasy Neale had him room with Pihos in order to be a calming influence on the rookie. One Saturday night, Sears recounted, they were in their room when Pihos got a hankering for the early edition of Sunday's newspaper. "Sears, go get the paper," he told him.

"Pihos, why the hell should I go get the paper?" the veteran tackle replied.

"I'm Pihos, that's why."

"I'm Sears, that's why I'm not going."

Still, it was clear early on that the brash rookie had talent. He played end in the pros, but Pihos gave his teammates and opponents the feeling that he could play just about any position. "Pete was a technician, a hard worker. He felt every play, he had to make every play. And he was awfully good at it," recalled Gordy Soltau, a San Francisco end who in 1952 would be named to the same All-Pro squad as Pihos. (Pihos was selected six times in his nine-year career.)

On offense, Pihos was sure-handed, fearless, and hard-to-tackle; on both offense and defense he was rugged, aggressive, and prone to make big plays. "He was the sort of guy," commented a columnist of the day, "you'd expect to buy a piano and promptly carry it home."

In selecting Pihos as the greatest tight end of all time, coach George Allen wrote, "He was no giant, but he was big enough. He was no sprinter, but he was fast enough. He was extremely tough and durable and determined, and he seemed to me an exceptionally smart player. He was the kind of player coaches like me wanted to captain their clubs."

"Pihos," said *The Sports Encyclopedia: Pro Football,* "blocked like an

11403-COHE

avalanche, hugged every pass like a falling baby, and joined Jack Ferrante in the toughest end combination in the league."

Pihos and Ferrante made something of an unlikely tandem. In 1947, there were 14 men playing in either the NFL or the AAFC who had not played college football. One was Eagles guard Dusan "Duke" Maronic. Too light to play college ball, he had started out playing semipro ball in the steel country of Pennsylvania, playing at one point on what was otherwise an all-black team. By the mid-Forties, he had bulked up and established himself. He joined the Eagles in 1944, having been recommended for a tryout by the sports editor of a local newspaper. Another was Joe Sulatis, a jack-of-all-trades who played for the New York Giants for 10 of his 11 NFL seasons. And then there was Jack Ferrante, one of the few men in the history of professional football who played neither college nor high school football.

Ferrante came out of the sandlot leagues of South Philadelphia. He was born in Camden, N.J., in 1916, and his family moved across the Delaware River to Philadelphia in 1923. In the mid Thirties, with the weight of the Depression on his family, he left school to work full time. In his spare time, he played football. In 1934, Ferrante, then a teen, hooked up with a neighborhood athletic club called Rockne.

"I wouldn't say (it was) professional because I don't think anybody got paid. . . . That first year that I played, it was a new neighborhood that I moved into. I asked people if I could play with somebody around the neighborhood; they directed me to the team called Rockne," Ferrante recalled.

"We had eight or 10 teams in the league and we played Wednesday nights. Then on Sundays, we played independent ball. . . . That's where we made our money."

He spent 1935 to 1938 with another neighborhood athletic club, called Seymour. Given the state of pro football in Philadelphia at that time, semipro teams could draw as many fans as the Eagles, and Ferrante soon found himself with something of a following. In 1939, some friends of Ferrante's coaxed Bert Bell, who was then coaching the Eagles, to give him a tryout. Ferrante did not catch on with the team that year, but Walt Masters, a former Eagles back and major-league pitcher, saw

Ferrante and thought he had potential. Masters brought him to his Wilmington Clippers team in the American Association.

That league was a minor professional league, which served as a farm system for the NFL. The American Association was filled with young players like Ferrante, eager to make a strong impression and land in the NFL, as well as veteran players trying to cushion the blow on their way out of the NFL. There were also players who had been sent down for seasoning, often under the guidance of NFL veterans whose experience was valued. Allie Sherman, Augie Lio, and Angelo Bertelli were among those who would provide tutelage for Philadelphia's minor leaguers in the 1940s. Wilmington played twice a week, and players could make $50 or $75 a game.

"That year, I caught so many passes, I was the leading scorer, leading pass catcher. I made the all-star team," recounted Ferrante. He ended up in the league again in 1940, but he got a break in 1941: Greasy Neale wanted a look at him. The rookie coach liked what he saw, and the end had a job in the NFL. By then married to his childhood sweetheart, Connie, and expecting a child, Ferrante suddenly found himself with the chance to make $250 a game, plus a $250 signing bonus.

"Man, I grabbed it," Ferrante said.

As a 25-year-old rookie, the 6-foot-1, 205-pound Ferrante didn't have much success. He caught only two passes and found himself back in Wilmington for two more seasons. Then in 1944, with a talent at a premium because of the war, Ferrante returned to Neale's Eagles. This time, Ferrante caught three passes, including a touchdown.

The next year, he averaged 22.5 yards per reception and scored seven touchdowns. For the next few years, he was one of the NFL's more dangerous receivers. Neale sometimes started the game off with a long pass to Ferrante, hoping to throw his foe off track with a quick early strike. Longtime teammate Vic Sears said that Ferrante's success was simply a matter of Neale taking advantage of the considerable raw skills of a player who had learned how to get free and catch passes.

"He played the way he knew how to play," Sears said of Ferrante.

Ferrante was one of the steadier characters on the squad. A father of two, he continued to hold down second jobs, even during the season. During the war, he worked in defense-related jobs; after the war, he became a beer salesman and, later, a high school coach.

"Jack was one of the better people on the Eagles squad," recalled teammate Jim Parmer. "He was extremely friendly with everybody; everybody loved him. Jack would do things for the rookies that none of the rest of them would do. For instance, he would have us over to his house one time during the year and just stuff you full of the great Italian food until you couldn't possibly move, and you couldn't have got another bite down you. Jack worked all the time; when he played, he was a salesman for Ortleib's beer. I would imagine Jack was a great salesman because everybody liked him so much."

On the field, he was a valuable player both on offense and defense. He was also a bargain: As is true today, players like Ferrante who started at the low end of the team's wage scale could expect to get paid less throughout their careers than players who signed big contracts as rookies. As late as 1948, Ferrante was making less than at least half the other players on the Eagles, earning $6,250, the same as two backups, Noble Doss and Les Palmer. That year, Neill Armstrong was paid $7,500 and Pete Pihos $10,000.

Of course, Ferrante's path to the pros was rather unusual. But it was perfectly common for players to be discovered in haphazard ways.

The college draft, which had originated in 1936, was much more of a crapshoot than it is today. There are numerous stories about players being picked because the owner liked the way the person looked in a game program or thought he had a rugged-sounding name. Writer Tom Bennett said Greasy Neale and Eagles general manager Harry Thayer were laughed at when they showed up at the 1942 draft with 64 notebooks full of information on college players.

"Scouting wasn't sophisticated like it is now," longtime Eagles official Jim Gallagher told the Philadelphia Daily News when he retired in 1995. "Back then, we'd pay (college) coaches $50 to send us a list of the top players they saw that season. Some clubs drafted out of magazines. If a guy looked good in a picture, they'd take him."

Some of those draft stories may be exaggerations, but it's clear that the owners didn't treat drafting as a science, and the fans didn't treat the draft as big deal. This, for instance, is how the Associated Press described the NFL draft that took place Dec. 19, 1947:

"For the most part, the selections were from name schools but several of the clubs went into the minor leagues for little known players as they each picked approximately 30 men. Several of the club owners and coaches declined to name their complete lists, while the Steelers and Los Angeles Rams refused to divulge even a single name."

Today, almost every NFL organization talks about the need to build through the draft, but in the Forties, the process was viewed much differently. For one thing, coaches knew that they and they alone were apt to be familiar with local talent. Pro coaches could be expected to be familiar with the college all-Americans, but that might be the extent of their contact with prospects outside their area. One simply wouldn't expect teams in other cities to go scouring the bushes for hidden gems on college teams in your area. That's one reason why Paul Brown was able to stock his Browns with former Ohio high school stars, former Ohio State players, and former foes of his Ohio State squads, as well as players he had known from coaching the Bluejackets at Great Lakes.

The Eagles, too, had a local flavor. Ferrante, of course, had a local following. Frank "Bucko" Kilroy was a city boy who had played at Temple University; he would eventually be joined on the line by fellow Temple product Mike Jarmoluk. Later in the Forties, the team would add three University of Pennsylvania stars: tackle George Savitsky, back Frank Reagan, and center-linebacker Chuck Bednarik. Backup quarterback Bill Mackrides grew up in Philadelphia and had served as the team's waterboy for a year. Linemen Duke Maronic and Baptiste Manzini were from other parts of Pennsylvania. Bringing in local players was not only a reasonable way to stock one's team, but also good business, because these players might well bring in their fans.

"I had a lot of people who were rooting for me because I was a hometown boy. No question about it," recalled Mackrides of his days with the Eagles. "They would yell, 'Put Mackrides in. Put Mackrides in.' I had a whole group of fans sitting up there."

That's not to say teams didn't want to bring in players from other areas. The all-American and all-conference teams were a good place for teams to start their search; that's certainly where the Eagles found Pihos, as well as fellow end Neill Armstrong, who led the nation in receptions in 1943 and 1946 while at Oklahoma A&M.

But when it came to bringing in players from other parts of the country, teams generally had only a faint idea of what they were getting. Tackle Vic Sears came to the Eagles sight unseen in 1941 after making a name for himself at Oregon State. Sears, whose playing weight at the time was just over 200 pounds, remembered the Eagles being disappointed when he showed up and they realized he was not a giant Oregon "woodsman."

These kind of surprises happened not only when players went from the college to the pros, but also when they were recruited by the colleges. Wally Triplett remembered getting an offer of an athletic scholarship from the University of Miami after making a high school all-star team in suburban Cheltenham, Pa. Triplett had to write back and inform the Florida school that he knew they could not make use of him because he was black. Instead, he went to Penn State and then on to the Detroit Lions. This whole process was much different than it is today, when high school stars become known to draft aficionados at age 17 or 18 and their progress is followed until they turn pro.

Moreover, even the nation's top college players did not follow a uniform path to the pros. Today one assumes that the lion's share of the nation's college stars become acquainted with football at an early age, play the game all through school, depart for college around the age of 18, and turn pro at the age of 21 or 22 or 23. In the 1940s, there was no telling what kind of background a player, even a blue-chip player, had. Tackle Al Wistert, for instance, had been an all-American at the University of Michigan, one of three Wistert brothers to achieve that honor for that college. But, like Ferrante, he had not played high school football.

"I didn't play in high school though because Mother was a widow– Father had been a police sergeant in Chicago and he was shot and killed by a holdup man in, he died in 1926, when I was 5 and a half years old," Wistert recounted. "Mother had six children to raise, three boys and three girls. And, so, we came to her with a slip of paper to sign for high school football–you know absolving the school from any responsibility if we got hurt. Then she'd say, 'Well, I can't sign that. What if you get hurt? I can't afford to pay doctor bills.' "

Instead Wistert, like Ferrante, joined an athletic club in a league for which he did not need the permission of his mother to play. Wistert's longtime Eagles linemate Vic Lindskog also took an unconventional route: He worked in oil fields for six years between high school and college, intent on becoming a petroleum engineer. Lindskog eventually gave up that hope and, after a solid gridiron career at Stanford, entered the NFL in 1944 at the age of 28.

Others spent long stretches in the military before turning pro: Hall-of-Famer Richard "Night Train" Lane came to the NFL in 1952 at the age of 24. He played briefly at Scottsbluff Junior College in the late Forties and then spent four years in the military. Despite having almost no college experience, Lane went on to set the NFL's interception record in his rookie year. West Point's legendary Glenn Davis did not turn pro until 1950, and his backfield mate, Doc Blanchard, never played in the NFL. Segregation and military service kept Rams end Woody Strode out of an NFL game until he was 32. Because of these types of detours, it was not uncommon in the late Forties and early Fifties for rookies to be in their late 20s or early 30s.

The most extreme case was that of Otis Whitfield Douglas. This Virginian, said Eagles back Jim Parmer, "should have been a mountain man, he should have lived back in the 1700s. Could do anything in the way of a boat, handling a canoe, swimming, diving; anything like that Otis Douglas could do." Yet, somehow, he ended up in the NFL.

Douglas had played tackle for John Kellison, Neale's longtime line coach, at William and Mary from 1929 to 1931. After graduation, he took up coaching, boxing, wrestling, and semipro football. Douglas also got a master's degree in physical education, ran a fishing business with his brother and operated a camp for boys in Virginia. At the start of World War II, he enlisted and became a pilot.

In 1946, Kellison brought Douglas to the Eagles as a trainer, but a rash of injuries forced him into uniform at tackle. He was 35 years old. At that time, there was only one player in the National Football League who was older, Giants kicker Ken Strong. By 1948, Douglas was the oldest player in the NFL.

For four seasons, he split duties between the field and the training table, serving also as head coach of the college team at nearby Drexel, as well as a wrestler, pilot, carpenter, plumber, and whatever else he could make time for. "First man on practice field," said an Eagles 1949 team program of Douglas. "Sometimes leads calisthenics . . . first man in dressing room before game . . . tapes ankles, etc., before players leave for field." Today, a player with Douglas' background would probably be celebrated as an amazing novelty. In the Forties, amazing novelties were a dime a dozen.

*****

The same day that the Eagles outlasted the Redskins, there were two other memorable NFL contests. The champion Chicago Bears stumbled in their opener, losing to the Green Bay Packers, 29-20. Packers quarterback Jack Jacobs was the hero, passing for two touchdowns and scoring a third in the waning seconds of the game. Meanwhile, the lowly Chicago Cardinals showed that they were going to be a force to reckoned with, trampling Detroit Lions, 45-21. Pitchin' Paul Christman of the Cards completed 16 of 24 passes for a total of 320 yards.

In the next two weeks, the Cardinals proved they were for real by beating the Bears, 31-7, and then the Packers, 14-10. The addition of Charley Trippi had given them an all-star backfield, and Christman had become a first-rate passer. "Chicago's flag-hungry Cardinals stand alone today as the only unbeaten major team in professional football and the one outfit holding undisputed possession of a divisional lead in either of the two big circuits," the Associated Press said after their win over Green Bay.

The Cardinals stumbled before an NFL record crowd of 69,631 in Los Angeles in the fourth game but then beat Boston, Los Angeles,

Detroit, and Green Bay to jump out to a 7-1 mark and first place in the NFL's West.

The Eagles, meanwhile, were erratic, particularly on defense. In the second game of the season, they shut down the Giants, 23-0, in Philadelphia. It was their second straight win over a division rival and boded well for their playoff chances. But in the third week, Sid Luckman and the winless Chicago Bears got untracked, pounding the Eagles, 40-7, in Chicago. Luckman completed 14 of 24 passes for 314 yards and three touchdowns, and end Ken Kavanaugh accumulated 144 yards on only two receptions.

Philadelphia stumbled again in the following game. On Oct. 19, the Eagles lost to Pittsburgh, 35-24, despite a stellar effort by Steve Van Buren, who carried the ball 21 times for 133 yards. The Steelers scored 21 late points to overcome a 10-point Philadelphia lead. Backs Steve Lach and Johnny Clement, known as "Johnny Zero" because of his preference for the numeral "0" on his jersey, were the heroes. At this point, the Eagles were 2-2, while Jock Sutherland's Steelers were in first place, at 3-2.

The Steelers proceeded to run off four straight wins, and the Eagles kept pace. First up for Philadelphia was the Rams. The Eagles won, 14-7, keeping Bob Waterfield and the Rams' offense off the board until the fourth quarter. On Nov. 2, they beat the Redskins again, 38-14. Van Buren was the star, carrying the ball 17 times for 138 yards and two touchdowns. The next week, the hero was fellow halfback Bosh Pritchard, who scored three times as the Eagles beat the Giants, 41-24, at the Polo Grounds. On Nov. 16, as Ferrante caught two touchdown passes, they posted their second shutout of the season in beating Boston, 32-0. The race between the cross-state rivals from Pennsylvania seemed destined to go down to the last week.

In the NFL's West, there were also two dominant teams, the upstart Cardinals from Chicago's South Side and their vaunted uptown rivals, the Bears. The Week 3 win over the Eagles seemed to get the mighty Bears back on track. Over the next seven games, the Bears outscored their opponents, 261-137. During this stretch, the Bears could seemingly do no wrong. On Oct. 26, hefty center-linebacker Bulldog Turner ran back an interception 96 yards against the Redskins. Against the Yankees a week later, Luckman threw two touchdown passes to Kavanaugh in the final five minutes for a dramatic 28-24 triumph.

The two divisions were thrown into disarray on Nov. 23 as three of the four contenders were beaten. Playing on Sammy Baugh Day in Washington, the Redskins stunned the Cardinals, 45-21. Baugh surpassed his spectacular opening-day performance against the Eagles, completing 25 of 33 passes for 355 yards and six touchdowns, one short of Sid Luckman's league record.

The Bears, meanwhile, battered the Steelers, 49-7, for their seventh straight win, while the Eagles fell to the Boston Yankees, 21-14. Yankees quarterback Boley Dancewicz threw two touchdown passes and scored a third TD to spark his team to their first-ever triumph over the Eagles. The Steelers remained a half-game ahead of the Eagles; the Bears and Cardinals were now tied.

The Eagles and Bears briefly both took command the following week. As the Cardinals were being upset, 35-31, by the Giants, the Bears blasted the Lions, 34-14, to take the division lead. In Philadelphia, the Eagles shut out the Steelers, 21-0.

"Joe Muha spearheaded the Eagle triumph by scoring one touchdown and setting up another with a 59-yard quick kick before a record Shibe Park crowd of 39,814 fans," said the Associated Press account. "The Steelers, playing without their injured star back, Johnny Clement, threatened only once."

But the Bears and Eagles could not close the door on their pursuers. The following week, The Rams, foundering at 4-6, upset the Bears, 17-14. The Cardinals, meanwhile, blew the doors off the Eagles.

"Trailing 7-3 at the end of the half, the visiting Cards exploded for six touchdowns in the second half to rout the Eagles and tie the Bears for the Western lead," The Associated Press reported Dec. 8. "The defeat dropped the Eagles into second place, a half-game behind the Pittsburgh Steelers, who vaulted to the top after their 17-7 win over the Boston Yanks. The Steelers have completed their schedule and the Eagles must whip the Packers to stay in the picture. An Eagle triumph over the

Packers will deadlock the Eastern half race and necessitate a playoff for the title."

For the Eagles, the 45-21 defeat was a devastating display of the power of the Cardinals' offense. Charley Trippi and end Mal Kutner each scored two touchdowns, while back Pat Harder scored one touchdown, kicked a field goal, and made six extra points. The Cardinals' momentum carried over to the following week as they faced the Bears for the division title.

Paul Christman hooked up with halfback Boris "Babe" Dimancheff for an 80-yard touchdown pass on the first play from scrimmage. Cardinals coach Jimmy Conzelman had been planning the play all week, but had been unable to practice it, since Dimancheff spent the week at his wife's side waiting for her to deliver a baby. On the play, Dimancheff beat Bears linebacker Mike Holovak and broke free, but scored only after briefly stumbling over Wrigley Field's pitching mound.

After that initial score, Elmer Angsman added two more touchdowns as the Cardinals jumped out to a 27-7 lead and held on to win, 30-21. They had intercepted Bears quarterback Sid Luckman four times in posting their most significant win over their crosstown rivals. It was their first Western title.

That same day, the Eagles showed their mettle by beating Green Bay, 28-14. Steve Van Buren scored three touchdowns and racked up 96 yards for a new NFL rushing record of 1,008 yards. Pete Pihos also had a big day, catching four passes for 108 yards. The victory was the franchise's first over Green Bay in 10 tries and set up a divisional playoff Dec. 21 with the Steelers.

Like the Eagles, the Steelers were trying to get to the championship game for the first time. In 1946, tailback Bill Dudley had practically carried the team to a 5-5-1 record, but Dudley and coach Jock Sutherland didn't get along so Dudley ended up in Detroit in 1947. After Dudley was traded, Sutherland was left with a relatively anonymous cast of characters and an old-style single wing offense. But John Bain "Jock" Sutherland was perhaps the toughest taskmaster the NFL had ever seen; writer Robert Leckie called him "grim and relentless" and "a close-mouthed tiger of a man from the Scottish heather."

Sutherland, who had made his name by winning more than 80 percent of his games while coaching at Lafayette and the University of Pittsburgh from 1919 to 1938, molded this Steelers team into a solid unit. Johnny Clement took over at tailback for Dudley, but there was no one else who could be considered a real star.

The divisional playoff game was at Forbes Field in Pittsburgh, but the Eagles quickly established their superiority. In the first quarter, Pete Pihos blocked a punt.

"I knew we were beaten then," Sutherland told the Associated Press after the game. "One of our tackles failed to block Pihos, letting him through to jam Bob Cifers' kick."

Two plays later, Tommy Thompson threw to Steve Van Buren for a 15-yard touchdown, and Cliff Patton converted the extra point. In the second quarter, Thompson threw a 28-yard touchdown to Jack Ferrante to give the Eagles a 14-0 lead. "The Eagles threat of quick kicks by (Joe) Muha also pulled our safety man out of position time and again– a factor which Tommy Thompson used to advantage in calling pass plays," Sutherland said afterward.

In the third quarter, Bosh Pritchard scored on a 79-yard punt return, and the Eagles went on to win, 21-0. On the day, Thompson completed 11 of 18 passes for 131 yards, and Ferrante caught five passes. Greasy Neale's defense was superb. Pittsburgh passers Johnny Clement and Bob Cifers could only complete four of the 18 passes they attempted, and the Steelers were held to seven first downs. Clement had one 27-yard run, but he was otherwise rendered ineffective.

"The game had been expected to develop into a bruising battle between two teams that a few years ago were so weak that they were combined using the name of the Steagles. Instead it was a gallop for the Eagles as they went into the finals against a club that also was once a league doormat," said the Associated Press.

For Sutherland, it was an unfortunate finale. He was hospitalized in April 1948 and died of a brain tumor a few days later. Assistant coach John Michelosen took over for Sutherland, but Art Rooney's starless Steelers fell to 4-8 in 1948 and didn't play in another playoff game until 1972.

*****

The Cardinals were the opposite of the Steelers: They were loaded with stars. Before his death in early 1947, owner Charles W. Bidwill Sr. had spent generously to acquire a collection of former all-Americans. Seven of his players had such stellar collegiate careers that they eventually ended up in college football's hall of fame: Center Vince Banonis, guard Garrard "Buster" Ramsey, end Mal Kutner, and backs Marshall "Biggie" Goldberg, Marlin "Pat" Harder, Pitchin' Paul Christman, and, of course, Charley Trippi.

The pride and joy of the Cardinals was their backfield, which was known as the "Dream Backfield." In 1947, Christman was the quarterback, and Harder the fullback, as well as the place-kicker. At halfback were Trippi and Goldberg, a veteran from the University of Pittsburgh who at one point had been the NCAA's all-time leading rusher. They were joined at the position by Elmer Angsman, an explosive 22-year-old from Notre Dame who was already in his third season in the league. On the bench there were other weapons: Ray Mallouf, Bill DeCorrevont, and Babe Dimancheff, whose big catch had stunned the Bears in their final-week showdown. "It was the type of football team," Trippi was quoted as saying in *The Running Backs*, "where the pressure wasn't only on one man."

The team had some stars in its front wall too: Ramsey, Banonis, and Stan Mauldin were well-regarded linemen, and Kutner had led the NFL in receiving yardage at end. Their coach was Jimmy Conzelman, who had a been a standout player-coach in the early days of the NFL, playing quarterback for George Halas' Decatur Staleys in the first season of the league.

"Jimmy Conzelman was a wonderful guy, and he was very imaginative," recounted Marshall Goldberg. "He was quite a personality and very clever, and he got the most out of the boys."

Conzelman, then 49, was a colorful character. He was dubbed "Jimmy of the silvery hair, twinkling fingers, and infectious humor" by writer Howard Roberts.

"There was a time," asserted the International News Service in an article Dec. 30, "when Conzelman seemed to take his football coaching as a sort of side dish. His main interests were after-dinner speech-making on the rubber-chicken circuit, writing for the magazines, and playing tap-room pianos until all hours of the morning. He still pursues those varied avocations, but when he suddenly found himself with a good ballclub, instead of the humpty-dumpty of those other years, he got down to business with the talent at hand.

"Going into the title game, Conzelman saw the Eagles as a tough foe. "No doubt about it that they're the class of the East," he told the Associated Press after attending the Eagles-Steelers divisional playoff game with Christman, Mallouf, and three of his assistants. "They are rough and tough and will be hard to stop. But I'm sure we'll be up for this one."

The Cardinals also had special incentive to win this one. During the season, rookie Jeff Burkett had suffered an attack of appendicitis while the team was in California to play the Rams. He recuperated and then boarded a plane home. Burkett's plane crashed in Utah, killing the 26-year-old from Louisiana State. Now the Cardinals were playing both for the memory of Bidwill and Burkett.

Conzelman and his team were confident. The extra week that the Cardinals had off while the Eagles played the Steelers for the divisional crown had given Harder, Trippi, and Ramsey time to recuperate from injuries. The Cardinals also drew confidence from their 45-21 regular-season win and an exhibition game victory in Buffalo on Sept. 5. They were playing at home and favored by 10 to 12 points.

The Eagles, for their part, figured that Tommy Thompson, Steve Van Buren, Bosh Pritchard and Joe Muha were fully a match for the Dream Backfield. Their 5-2-4 defense had led the NFL in defense against the run, giving them hope of stopping Trippi and company. Also, the team was healthy; only backup halfback Noble Doss was banged up.

There was, however, one factor that neither team had counted on: Ice. On the day of the championship game, Comiskey Park was frozen solid.

"The field was beautiful the day before," recounted Eagles end-defensive back Dick Humbert. "We got there and the grass was just soft . . . Oh man, it was beautiful. And when we came out for the game, (we discovered that) they had pulled the tarp off the night before and the field froze."

"Honestly, you could not walk across the field without falling down," recalled backup quarterback Bill Mackrides.

Before the game, the Eagles opted to have the cleats of everyone (except kicker Cliff Patton) sharpened to improve traction. What happened next is a matter of some contention. Here are four theories:

1.) Humbert recalled that Greasy Neale got permission for the Eagles to use shoes with sharpened cleats, only to have the same official that approved the shoes penalize the Eagles for illegal equipment after the game started.

2.) Al Wistert said the trouble started when an official came into the locker room to give the team its five-minute warning and saw Bosh Pritchard filing his cleats down. Once the game started, the officials started checking the Eagles for illegally sharpened shoes.

3.) Vic Lindskog said that the officials saw the Eagles were getting better traction than the Cardinals and started checking their shoes.

4.) Jack Ferrante said that it was simply a matter of the officials responding to the complaint of a Chicago player who had been cut by the sharpened shoes.

Whatever the situation, their shoes were too sharp to suit the officials. The Eagles found themselves getting penalized for illegal equipment on their first offensive series and having to scrounge for tennis shoes to wear. With the substitution rules being what they were, the Eagles could not send everyone out for one play and bring them back on the next play. Instead, they had to shuttle a couple players at a time in and out. The players then had to get used to their new footwear.

"We had to go–omigod it was a mess–the trainer had to go in and get all new ones and everything else and change. It was terrible," Ferrante said.

The Cardinals, who were wearing sneakers from the start, had a distinct early advantage and they capitalized on it. After receiving an Eagles punt, they sent Charley Trippi up the middle and he ran 44 yards for a touchdown. In the second quarter, they ran a very similar play with Elmer Angsman. He went 70 yards for a score. Pat Harder converted both extra points to give Chicago a 14-0 lead.

Good footing was not the only factor here. The Cardinals had found a weakness in the Eagles' 5-2-4 defense. They realized that if the middle guard could be moved out of the way, the middle of the field would be open. On both of those touchdown runs, the Cardinals double-teamed the middle guard and sent their backs to daylight, knowing that the Eagles would have a heckuva time catching them in the open field. Eagles defensive back Ernie Steele remembered the game as one in which he spent the whole day sliding across the field chasing Trippi.

On offense for the Eagles, Steve Van Buren was struggling, but Tommy Thompson brought the Eagles to life in the second quarter. Near the end of the first half, he completed a 53-yard touchdown to rookie back Pat McHugh. Cliff Patton's extra point cut the lead at halftime to 14-7. But Charley Trippi opened the lead up to 14 again in the third quarter, taking a punt and going 75 yards for a score. This spectacular run cemented the rookie's already growing legend.

"He grabbed a punt on his own 25-yard line," wrote Murray Olderman years later, "and started down the right sideline. At the Eagles' 30, he skidded, staggered like a tightrope walker, then slipped again 10 yards further down but regained his balance and sprinted into the end zone for a 75-yard run."

After Van Buren had cut the margin to 21-14 with a short touchdown run, the Cardinals got another spectacular long run, this time by Angsman. Going through the center of the line once again, he ran 70 yards for a touchdown in the middle of the fourth quarter. The Eagles got a touchdown from Russ Craft to cut the margin to 28-21, but Cardinals veteran Marshall Goldberg snuffed out their final threat by intercepting a pass in the closing minutes.

What had started as a sluggish and slippery game produced some spectacular offensive performance. Paul Christman had been held to three pass completions in 14 attempts, but the Cardinals had compensated by rushing for 282 yards. Angsman had gained 159 yards, a championship game record, on 10 carries, and Trippi had provided two long runs. For the Eagles, Van Buren had been unable to do much, gaining only 26 yards on 18 carries, but Thompson set championship game records by completing 27 of 44 passes for 297 yards. Ferrante had caught eight of those passes, setting yet another mark.

The attendance, unfortunately, wasn't a record-setter. The crowd of 30,759 was the smallest at a title game since 1941, leaving net receipts of less than $120,000 for the players to divide up as their championship game earnings. For their victory, the Cardinals collected $1,132 each. The Eagles each got $754. Still, it was a spectacularly satisfying day for Jimmy Conzelman and the Cardinals.

"When I came with the Cardinals in 1939, they had nothing. And I stayed all the way through 'til we won the championship," recalled Goldberg. "The Cardinals were an exciting ballclub in '46, '47, '48. Really the outstanding team in the league over those three years. It was a happy organization."

4

1948—THE GAME OF THEIR LIVES

****

"After the '47 season when we came back, we were so disappointed that we didn't win the championship," Al Wistert recalled. "The management of Old Bookbinder's restaurant went to the Eagles coaching staff or management and said, 'Hey, what can we do to help out here, we'd like to do something?' And out of that came a plan."

Neale presented that plan to the team, According to Wistert, the coach said, " 'Hey listen: Old Bookbinder's restaurant says if we can shut an opponent out, that they will invite the whole team as their guest to Old Bookbinder's restaurant for whatever we want to eat.' Now that's quite a deal. But listen, they didn't only extend this to the players but to the player and his wife and his children; the coaches, their wives, and their children."

The offer from Bookbinder's, one of Philadelphia's great restaurants, had a great ring to it, but there was no guarantee that it would help the team do what it so badly wanted to do: Erase those images of Charley Trippi and Elmer Angsman galloping through the center of the line. Greasy Neale sorted out the problem and came up with his own solution. What the defense needed, he figured, was more bulk in the center of the line. So, for the 1948 season, he brought in two rookie behemoths.

One was Walter "Piggy" Barnes, a 30-year-old Army veteran from Neale's hometown in West Virginia. Barnes weighed 240 pounds and was one of the very few linemen in the NFL who lifted weights. The other was Mario "Yo-Yo" Giannelli of Boston College. A former boxer, he weighed 270 pounds. A 1949 Eagles game program described him simply as "difficult to hurt."

Neale's idea was that the added strength would keep foes from opening a hole in the center of his line. The addition of Barnes, Giannelli, and fellow rookies John Magee and George Savitsky gave Neale much-needed depth, making it possible for him to make sure that his linemen did not get worn out. A 1948 game program, describing the team's increasingly formidable "brawn trust," said, "The Eagles really struck a jackpot this year in coming up with exceptional material to bolster the line."

The new linemen got a quick test. On Friday Sept. 24 at Chicago's Comiskey Park, the Eagles and Cardinals squared off in the season opener. It was a rugged contest, and the outcome–another win by the Cardinals–would be overshadowed by tragedy.

"Trippi, who usually carries the ball, brought the Cards victory with a last-period touchdown pass that covered 64 yards," the Associated Press wrote. "Tied at 14-14 in the final four minutes of play, Trippi took a hand-off, faked a wide end run, and then made a leaping toss. The ball landed in the arms of Mal Kutner 31 yards away and Kutner scrambled the remaining distance to paydirt."

At the end of the game, Cardinals tackle Stan Mauldin helped Eagles center-linebacker Alex Wojciechowicz off the field. At 27, Mauldin was at the top of his game, a three-year veteran from the University of Texas by way of the 15th Air Force Division. The two formidable linemen had battled each other all night, and both were hurting: "Wojie" had hurt his back, Mauldin had a splitting headache. When he dropped Wojciechowicz off at one of Comiskey Park's dugouts, Mauldin ran off–probably, Wojie figured, to throw up.

"I was taking a shower when I got the word that Stan Mauldin was in the Cardinal locker room unconscious," Wojciechowicz told writer Myron Cope. "I hurried over there, and when I entered that locker room, my God, Stan was stretched out on the rubbing table and they had oxygen on his face. Some of the ballplayers were in the nude and some were completely dressed, and all of them were kneeling around that table. They were praying. There was not a sound in the room. Half an hour later, Stan died."

Greasy Neale was quoted in news accounts as saying that the league had lost its "greatest tackle." Mauldin's death was initially reported to have been from a hemorrhage, but it was later discovered that he suffered a heart attack. No one knows why.

"The victory," said the Associated Press in its game story, "was marred by the death in the dressing room shortly after the game of the Cardinals' first-string tackle, Stan Mauldin. Mauldin, 27, collapsed after the game and died two hours later."

*****

Tragedies such as the death of Stan Mauldin have been rare in pro football. Five men–Mauldin, Dave Sparks, Howard Glenn, Stone Johnson, and Chuck Hughes–have died from injuries sustained in professional games. But football was and is a game of power and pain. Those who play the sport are a fraternity of men whose mission it is to hit and be hit. And most of the members of this fraternity do not get the glory involved in throwing or catching or running with the ball. For those whose job it is to block and tackle, there is a life of relative anonymity.

In recent years, more of these men have gotten famous than ever before, not just outstanding players like Reggie White and Deion Sanders, but also characters such as William "The Refrigerator" Perry and Brian Bosworth. In the Eighties, Fifties star Art Donovan got much more attention for telling funny stories about the years *when men were men* than he ever got for playing. In pro football's formative years, the grunts of the game were relatively faceless.

During the glory years of the Eagles, Neale's team had an

outstanding collection of linemen and linebackers. These players were revered by the team's most devoted fans, but that was the extent of their fame. Perks, such as free meals at Bookbinder's, came only to them when they came to the team as a whole. When they did their jobs, when they made the block or the tackle, it was assumed that they were merely doing what pro football players were supposed to do.

These are capsule looks at the seven men whom the Eagles of 1948 counted on to be their best blockers and their leading tacklers:

FRANK KILROY–A Philadelphia boy who joined the Eagles in 1943. Served in the Navy. Started at tackle; moved to guard in 1947. One of the larger players in the NFL in his time, playing at 270 pounds or so. Al Wistert credited him with teaching him some key blocking techniques. Known for his speed and known as a particularly vicious hitter; came under much criticism over the years for his play. Born Francis Joseph; acquired the nickname "Bucko" in the late Forties. Famous quote: "We were raised to love your God, respect your elders, and fear no son-of-a-bitch that walks."

VIC LINDSKOG–Drafted in the second round in 1942, he joined the Eagles out of Stanford in 1944 at the age of 28. Former boxer. A lightweight center, playing at just over 200 pounds. Chicago All-Pro Bulldog Turner, at one point, called him the best center in the league. Known for his down-field blocking and his studious approach to the game. Led the team in calisthenics. Retired after 1947 season to coach, but was coaxed back. Owned an oil and water well drilling company in Montana.

JOE MUHA–First-round draft choice from VMI who joined team in 1946 after serving in Marines. 6-foot-1, 205 pounds. Played fullback and linebacker. Also punted and kicked long field goals; he led the NFL in punting in 1948 and was famous for his surprise "quick kicks" out of standard offensive formations. Probably the team's leading tackler during this era. A civil engineer who designed homes, Muha was a deep thinker to whom his teammates came for advice.

CLIFF PATTON–Texan of Indian-Irish descent who joined the team in 1946. Army veteran. 6-foot-2, 240 pounds. Guard and supremely accurate kicker; at one point held NFL record (84) for consecutive extra points made. Good-natured. A beer lover, he worked himself into shape each training camp. Given name is John. Quote: "The players accepted me and helped me grow into wisdom that they already had."

VIC SEARS–Joined team from Oregon State in 1941 after being drafted by Steelers. Tackle. 6-foot-3. Entered league at 208 pounds; gained about 20 pounds or so over the duration of his career. Tough, sturdy and dependable. Missed 1944 season with a leg injury. Quiet off the field; Jim Parmer recalled that he had the bearing of a preacher.

AL WISTERT–Joined team from Michigan in 1943; fifth-round draft pick. Tackle. Like Lindskog, he was barely over 200 pounds. Very fast, standout down-field blocker. Captain of the team and an acknowledged leader. Perennial All-Pro. Frequent after-dinner speaker. Coached high school football in New Jersey in his spare time. Known as "Whitey" and "The Ox." Quote: "I did all I could to promote team spirit–that's what wins at any level."

ALEX WOJCIECHOWICZ–Legendary member of Fordham's "Seven Blocks of Granite" in the Thirties. Center and linebacker, but he mostly played defense for the Eagles after being acquired from Detroit in 1946. Called signals on defense. Rugged, known for his ability to hammer receivers at line of scrimmage. Given name was Alexander Francis; nickname was "Wojie." Son of a Polish-immigrant tailor; expert at knitting. Teammate Jack Hinkle once described him as looking like a "sad-eyed St. Bernard."

There were others, of course. Thirty-seven men played for the Philadelphia Eagles in 1948, and the majority of them toiled in relative anonymity, as did hundreds of other players around the NFL and AAFC. But since football, as coaches and TV announcers are still fond of saying, has always been a game of blocking and tackling, these seven men were the heart and soul of the Philadelphia Eagles in 1948. And being the heart and soul of the Eagles meant something back then, something that went beyond winning and losing games. The Eagles were truly a team in every sense of the word. Being the heart and soul of the Eagles meant that you were at the center of a whole lifestyle, one that revolved around football but did not end when the game was over.

"The best thing they had," recalled Bucko Kilroy of those Eagles teams, "was great togetherness."

"In the last 15, 20 years," said Kilroy, a longtime official with the New England Patriots, "I watched them, you know there are a couple guys that are buddies or maybe three or four of them. This was a crew that they all traveled together. We didn't make any money, but we had a lot of fun."

Of course, the circumstances were different then. A player in 1948 spent less time on the field than he does today. The NFL season was considerably shorter, beginning in mid-September and lasting until early December. The playoffs were usually over by Christmas; it would have been unthinkable for the season to end after the New Year's Day bowl games in college football. Early in the season, the pro teams might be forced to play on weeknights to accommodate baseball. The Eagles, who played at Shibe Park, were one of several teams who played in a stadium whose main tenant was a baseball team.

Physically, players were significantly different. Training, before and during the season, had a different feel than it does now. It was not yet treated as if it were a science.

There was less emphasis on speed than there is now–though every coach was happy to have fast players–and less emphasis on appropriate weights for players, though players would certainly be told to lose weight if they were too fat. Players, however, didn't bulk up. In 1948, there were linemen as big as 290 pounds (the listed weight for Ed Neal of Green Bay), but if a player like Al Wistert showed that he could play tackle at 205 pounds, the coaches would live with that.

"They never had weight training in those days either. Or supplemental foods," recalled Vic Lindskog, who said that he and Wistert were the smallest linemen in the league. "Well, we ate a lot at training table but that didn't help."

Players from that era talk about both anabolic steroids and weight-lifting as being alien to their football experience. Walter Barnes was an exception; he lifted weights. Before joining the Eagles, Barnes had been a champion lifter in college who was seeking to qualify for the Olympics in 1948, but an injury derailed those hopes. "He gives lifting credit for much of his football proficiency," wrote Frank O'Gara in 1949, "and defends it against the charges that it makes one muscle-bound."

The notion that lifting weights would make one muscle-bound kept most of Barnes' contemporaries from lifting. Today that stigma is gone. Vic Sears, for instance, said he never lifted weights as a player, but did when he got older. When asked to compare players from the Forties with today's players, former San Francisco 49ers quarterback Frankie Albert noted, "Current players work on their bodies year round–as a result the linemen 'lift iron' without *any speed loss whatsoever*." (Emphasis is his.)

Steroids, though, are another matter.

"I'm glad I didn't have to go through steroids," said Lou Creekmur, a standout lineman for the Detroit Lions for 10 seasons. "When you think about it with steroids, I pity the poor kid who comes up, and he plays and he's 250 pounds, 6-foot-4. He plays against one guy who's about the same size, then the next year the opponent is 275, 280, with the muscles coming out of his ears. And he wonders, how's this happen? He finds out it's steroids. Well, in order for him to stay competitive, what's he gonna do. . . . He's gonna join the crowd. I'm glad that we didn't have those temptations when we were playing in the league."

Before the season, the NFL teams, as teams do today, held training camps. These camps tended to be different from team to team, depending on the coach. In 1946, for example, Pittsburgh's Jock Sutherland had perhaps the toughest training camp of all time, using relentless scrimmages every day to get the roster down from 110 players to 34. Guard Nick Skorich, then a rookie, told writer Stuart Leuthner that he spilled more blood in one particularly brutal scrimmage than he had in all of World War II. In his autobiography, Art Donovan described a similar training camp run by Clem Crowe with the 1950 Baltimore Colts. Crowe scrimmaged players constantly and to cap things off, Crowe made his final roster cuts as the players came off the plane after their final exhibition game.

With the Eagles, Greasy Neale held his training camps at a variety of sites over the years. During wartime, they were held nearby in such places as Hershey, Pa.; after the war, the team trained at such exotic locations as the University of Minnesota School of Agriculture in Grand Rapids, Minn. Neale strived more for quality than quantity in his practices, so he was not averse to canceling one now and again if it seemed like a good afternoon for golf or for the racetrack. His team's training methods were unconventional in other ways as well.

"Touch football! We played an hour of touch football each day before the coaches ever came out on the field for the practice sessions," recalled Al Wistert. "So we had our physical workout all done before they ever showed up. And we played a lot of touch football. Just to have a good time. This was good for team morale, playing, competing against one another . . . And it was great for the physical condition of the team."

However, Neale, perfectionist that he was, did ride his players hard; Steve Van Buren recounted that he was convinced every year that Neale was going to cut him. There was not much chance of *that* happening, though the competition for some jobs could be fierce. Jim Parmer remembered being a rookie in 1948, trying to win a job at the same time that veteran back Ben Kish was trying to keep his.

"Ben, I think, was a fine football player out of the University of Pittsburgh. By the time I got up there, Ben was getting a little old," Parmer recounted.

"Our offense was hard to learn because it was rote memory," he recalled. "You couldn't really make heads or tails out of it–we just worked on it so long that you finally remembered what you did. I can remember a lot of times, Kish would be standing by me when I was in the huddle and he would say, 'Go to the right' and if I did, I was in trouble, it was 'Go to the left.' "

Both Kish and Parmer made the roster that year. But, as Parmer's anecdote shows, a rookie could not expect any help from the veterans when it came to making the team. With players as close as they were in those years, rookies were a threat to a team's fellowship.

"There was a little bit of a rookie caste system, and I think it was kind-of beginning, as I hear, to ease up a little bit," said Parmer. "Veterans weren't near as hard on rookies as I understand they used to be before I went up. There were a few people who didn't speak much to the rookies and didn't really have anything to do with them. They were kind-of a necessary evil, I think, as far as they were concerned. But most of the veterans at least treated you fairly."

At a certain point, of course, winning games became the main concern of veterans and rookies alike. During the preseason, there were exhibition games (there might be six or more each season) and some of them were a big deal. Every year, the Philadelphia Inquirer sponsored a charity game that drew tremendous crowds: Both the 1945 and 1946 games drew more than 90,000 fans. The outstanding player in that game even got a special award, the Robert J. French Memorial Trophy. For exhibition games, teams would often venture to cities that didn't have NFL teams, and these games would often draw big crowds as well. The biggest of the exhibition games was the annual game between college all-stars and the defending NFL champion.

Once the regular season started, Greasy Neale and many of the Eagles players took up residence at hotels in the city. The Eagles players from the Forties speak of two: the Penn Sheraton on 39th and Chestnut Streets, and The Walnut Park Plaza at 63rd and Walnut.

"With the salaries we were getting," recalled Jack Ferrante, "they had to take the cheapest place they could go to. If they would get a group, the management would give them a cheaper rate."

These hotels functioned as a football neighborhood. Most of the players were married and many had children, so the hotels had something of a family atmosphere. Cliff Patton remembered being supplied by the hotel he lived in with milk and diapers when his children were born. Ernie Steele recounted taking his twin daughters out for Halloween with Al Wistert and his twin daughters. The team even held picnics in Philadelphia's vast Fairmount Park.

Alcohol and hijinks were part of the environment, though none of the players spoke of them as being a huge part of their lives together. They did, however, speak glowingly of the camaraderie of these places.

"As many of 16 of the married players lived there, raised our children, and enjoyed a great social life together," recalled Russ Craft of the Walnut Park Plaza. "We all have many fond memories of those days."

"My first three years," recounted Mario Giannelli, "I lived at the

Penn Sheraton Hotel. . . . Greasy Neale lived there. My roommate was Duke Maronic the first two years.

"My third year, 1950, I got married to a girl back home. . . . We lived at the Penn-Sheraton 1950. My last year, 1951, we rented a home on the outskirts of Philadelphia."

Not everyone on the team lived at these hotels, and these players were not without their disagreements. Still, the roles of the players on the team were often echoed by the roles they played in this football neighborhood in which they lived. Players who were leaders on the field were also leaders off of it. For instance, Joe Muha, who lived at the Walnut Park Plaza with his wife, Helen, was a guiding force for his teammates.

"In talking with Russ Craft, I found out that he could remember being counseled by Joe Muha," said Al Wistert, who gave Muha's eulogy after he died of cancer in 1993. "He said a lot of the players went to Joe because they thought that he was such a strong person and a level-headed person and an intelligent person. And so they would often go to him for counseling on personal matters or financial matters and so on."

For the players of this era, this sort of camaraderie took the place of more material rewards. The top-paid player (probably Bill Dudley or the AAFC's Glenn Dobbs) in the late Forties was earning around $20,000. This was in an era when the highest-paid players in baseball (Bob Feller, Joe DiMaggio, Hank Greenberg) could earn as much as $100,000, and movie stars could earn several hundred thousand–Bette Davis made $364,000 in 1948, about half of what movie mogul Louis B. Mayer, the highest-paid man in America, earned. For the 1948 film "Fort Apache," stars John Wayne, Henry Fonda, and Shirley Temple earned $100,000 each, while character actor Ward Bond was paid $25,000.

On the other hand, the average American industrial worker (according to statistics reported Jan. 1, 1948, by the Associated Press) earned $1.25 per hour; the minimum wage was raised from 40 cents to 75 cents an hour in 1949. Woody Strode recounted that he felt lucky because at the time that he was making $350 a week playing for the Rams, Los Angeles policemen were making $200 a month and firemen only $170.

Most pro football players made less than $10,000 per year playing football; on the 1948 Eagles, the only players who earned more than $10,000 were Steve Van Buren ($13,000), Tommy Thompson ($11,000), and Joe Muha ($12,500). According to *The Pro Football Chronicle*, no lineman in the NFL made more than $10,000 and some made as little as $4,000.

Players in the championship game divvied up the profits from that contest, but that put them at the mercy of attendance, which could be hurt by bad weather. Overall, there was not much in the way of security, since few contracts were guaranteed. About two-thirds of the players worked in the offseason; some also held second jobs during the season.

The number of perks associated with pro football were limited as well. Players did get to see the country: In the mid-Forties, teams even began using airplanes. Eagles lineman Baptiste Manzini remembered it as a highlight of his career when the team flew to Buffalo in 1945 on two transport planes for an exhibition game. Train travel, however, was much more common. "We would all meet at the train station and travel together to New York; Pittsburgh; Washington, D.C.; Boston; Chicago; etc. and return as soon as possible likewise," recounted Eagles end Neill Armstrong.

Newspaper coverage was limited. Professional football often took a back seat to college ball, high school ball, and, during the early part of the season, baseball. There was not much in the way of endorsements; Steve Van Buren was the most marketable commodity the Eagles had, and he apparently wasn't very interested in endorsing products. And there was no year-end Pro Bowl in Hawaii to call attention to the game's top individual performers.

A player could, however, make a little extra money as an after-dinner speaker or a coach at a nearby school. And with television in its infancy, a player could hope that his family might actually see him play, even if there wasn't much hope of profiting significantly from the exposure. Marshall Goldberg of the Cardinals recalled working with a young broadcaster named Mike Wallace on a Chicago football TV show. Goldberg said that he was paid $62.50 a week for those efforts.

Another "reward" was nicknames, which were much more

universal than they are today. Some were ethnic in nature: Norm Van Brocklin was known as "The Dutchman" and Goldberg, a native of West Virginia, was sometimes called "The Hebrew Hillbilly." (He was also known as "Biggie" and "Mad Marshall.") Cleveland's Bill Willis became the first of several black players to be known as "Deacon," perhaps after bandleader Louis Jordan's popular Deacon Jones character.

Some nicknames were geographic, as in the case of Clyde "Smackover" Scott from Smackover, Ark. Others were descriptive, as in the cases of Dick "Banana Hands" Humbert and Elroy "Crazy Legs" Hirsch and Ray "Muscles" Bray. And then there were nicknames that connoted respect, such as Dante "Glue Fingers" Lavelli, George "One Play" McAfee, and Clyde "Bulldog" Turner. In the tradition of "The Galloping Ghost," big stars often had nicknames that served as titles, such as "The Bluefield Bullet," a name used for Bill Dudley, and "The Gray Ghost of Gonzaga," a moniker for Tony Canadeo.

The downside of the pro sport was injuries. Of course, football players have always faced injuries, but the nature of the risk was somewhat different in the Forties. For one thing, there was no artificial turf, no seams for players to get their legs trapped in and destroyed. One doesn't read much of serious leg injuries in the Forties, at least not of torn knee ligaments and such. Players did break their legs and ankles and toes; a Chicago Rockets rookie named Bill McArthur had to have part of his left leg amputated in 1946 after a particularly severe broken leg. But, career-ending injuries of that nature appear to have been extraordinarily unusual.

However, injuries to the face and head were very common. Until the Forties, most players wore leather helmets without any face masks. These did not do much to protect a player's head and face. Noses and jaws were broken all the time, teeth were knocked out, and a player could be put to sleep by a well-placed elbow:

–Al Wistert recalled a time when Bears end Ed Sprinkle hit Joe Muha "with an elbow and almost killed him, almost killed him, put him unconscious for half an hour."

–Bears great Clyde "Bulldog" Turner told writer Paul Zimmerman that Green Bay behemoth Ed Neal broke his nose five times.

–Bears end Ken Kavanaugh recalled a time when the Bears were trying to get Eagles linebacker Alex Wojciechowicz off his back. Coach George Halas used two backs to ambush him, knocking Wojciechowicz's teeth out.

"We ran the play again the following quarter. And did the same thing, and he was really hurting and bleeding and everything," recounted Kavanaugh.

"We ran it again later, in the second half. We lined up and he says, 'Here comes the play, here comes that play, look out!' And they did, they pounded him too," he said. "It didn't stop him from lining up in front of me, but he was getting the heck beat out of him anyway."

Though face masks did not gain wide acceptance until the mid-Fifties, plastic helmets came into use in the Forties, and, as they became more common, they changed the game somewhat. Prone to concussions, Eagles back Russ Craft recalled being a test subject for a type of plastic helmet.

"The old leather gear was little more than an old-fashioned winter cap. It was either the 1947 or 1948 season, I wore the first plastic gear made by the Riddell Company," Craft recounted. "I did not receive one concussion after that time. I guess you can say it saved my future, maybe my life."

The NFL was reluctant to accept plastic helmets, figuring, correctly, that they could be used as weapons. The league banned them in 1948 but reinstated them in 1949.

Other rules were different in the 1940s. Until 1948, there were only four officials, making it much easier for someone to blindside a player away from the flow of the play and get away with it. Also at this time, a ballcarrier could get back up after being knocked down, as long as he was not firmly in the grasp of an opponent. (Some of the most famous runs of people like Steve Van Buren and Charley Trippi would have been whistled dead after a short gain under today's rules.) Therefore, it was completely reasonable to pile on top of a ballcarrier to make sure he didn't get up. What would be considered unnecessary roughness today was simply good common sense in the Forties.

*****

The results of the second week of the season indicated that neither the Eagles nor the Cardinals had gotten over the tragic death of Stan Mauldin. On Oct. 3, the Eagles jumped out in front of the Rams on three first-half touchdown passes by Tommy Thompson, only to see Bob Waterfield rally the Rams to a 28-28 tie. Waterfield was spectacular, throwing three touchdown passes–including a 24-yard pass to end Jack Zilly in the last minute–kicking four extra points, intercepting a pass, and recovering a fumble. "The Eagles will never be able to explain what happened when they get home," a Philadelphia journalist wrote. It looked like it might be awhile before the team enjoyed any free meals at Bookbinder's.

The Cardinals, meanwhile, were beaten by the Bears, 28-17, at Comiskey Park. Coming on the heels of a 45-7 opening-day victory by the Bears over the Packers, this win suggested that the Bears were the team to beat in 1948. George Halas had improved his team considerably in the offseason, adding three blue-chip rookies.

To bolster what was already the league's most-honored line, Halas had signed George Connor of Notre Dame. Connor, a tackle, was given a no-cut contract by Halas after being named the first winner of the Outland Trophy, an award given to the best lineman in college football. To spell Sid Luckman at quarterback, Halas had signed Heisman Trophy winner Johnny Lujack of Notre Dame and fellow all-American Bobby Layne of Texas. Both were given huge contracts, though Lujack spent most of the 1948 season at defensive back and Layne spent most of it on the bench.

The Cardinals and Eagles, however, both quickly righted themselves and joined the Bears as the NFL's top franchises, the only three legitimate title contenders in the league. In fact, those three teams combined with the AAFC's two best squads (Cleveland and San Francisco) to post a collective mark of 56-7-1, while the other 13 teams in the two leagues managed to go 59-108-1. Only once did one of the five powerful teams lose to one of the 13 weaker squads. In 1948, there was not much question as to who the contenders were and who the pretenders were.

Quarterback Paul Christman was injured in the loss to the Bears, but the 1948 Cardinals proved to be a devastating offensive machine. On Oct. 17, they beat the Giants, 63-35; a week later, they defeated Boston, 49-27. Later in the season, there would be victories of 56-20 over Detroit and 42-7 over Green Bay.

Playing much of the year at quarterback, veteran Ray Mallouf of SMU threw 13 touchdown passes. The team's outstanding receiver was Mal Kutner, who caught 14 touchdown passes and ran for a 15th to lead the league. A big-play threat, Kutner averaged 23 yards per reception to once again lead the NFL in receiving yardage.

In the backfield, Elmer Angsman, Pat Harder, and Charley Trippi all had their best seasons. Angsman rushed for 638 yards and nine touchdowns, while Harder rang up six touchdowns, seven field goals, and 53 extra points for a league-leading 110 points. Trippi, meanwhile, led the league by averaging 5.4 yards per carry. He returned two punts for touchdowns and would have led the NFL in punt returns, except that he didn't have enough attempts to qualify. Between his carries and receptions and kick returns, he ended up gaining 1,485 yards overall and scoring 10 touchdowns.

By the time, the once-beaten Bears and once-beaten Cardinals squared off Dec. 12, the last day of the season, the Cardinals appeared unstoppable. The Cards scored two touchdowns during a six-minute spurt in the last period to win, 24-21, and set up another title game with the Eagles.

The Eagles, meanwhile, had done both the Cardinals and themselves a favor early in the season by handing the Bears their first loss. It came on Oct. 24 after the Eagles had let loose with consecutive 45-0 wins over the Giants (Oct. 10) and Redskins (Oct. 17). The victory over Washington, however, had been somewhat expensive in that it cost the team the services of Tommy Thompson, who separated his shoulder on the last play of the first half. For their showdown with the Bears, the Eagles had to turn to second-year man Bill Mackrides.

"With Thompson virtually crippled from an injury to his throwing arm," an Eagles program noted in 1949, "Coach Earle (Greasy) Neale had to call on Billy Boy to shoulder the big burden. Few fans expected much from this inexperienced lad, who had been the Eagles' mascot and a center at West Philadelphia High before going on to far-away fame as a passer at the University of Nevada."

Playing in a driving rain in Philadelphia, Mackrides drove the Eagles to one touchdown before being relieved by the injured Thompson in the fourth quarter. The Eagles also got a field goal by Cliff Patton and a safety by Walter Barnes to build a 12-7 lead. Mackrides finished things off by running out the clock.

"Greasy had me call quarterback sneaks to kill the clock. And three, I ran three, quarterback sneaks. They were ripping at me, picking me up, they had me up in the air, all over the place, trying to rip the ball out, out of my hands," recalled Mackrides.

Mackrides held on to the football, and the Eagles had their first victory over the Bears in 12 tries. The win provided a psychological boost to the team, which went through the next five weeks of its schedule like a blowtorch going through butter.

On Oct. 31, Tommy Thompson returned to the helm and completed 16 of 22 passes as the Eagles beat the Steelers, 34-7. That day, Steve Van Buren rushed for 109 yards on 22 carries, scoring one touchdown. The following week, Van Buren had the best day of his career, rushing for 143 yards and two touchdowns in a 35-14 win over Giants. Pete Pihos also had his best day as a professional, catching five passes for 128 yards and two touchdowns.

The Eagles got their third 45-0 victory of the season on Nov. 14. This one was over the Boston Yankees and it saw another stellar performance by Van Buren, who gained 137 yards on 16 carries.

On Nov. 21, Van Buren and Thompson did it again as the Eagles beat Washington, 42-21. Thompson passed for three touchdowns, while Van Buren set another new career high, carrying the ball for 171 yards. The Associated Press was so impressed by their 1-2 punch that it made point-by-point comparisons of the two to Cleveland's star duo.

"Two running-and-passing combinations that work together like beer and pretzels are bidding for attention in the rival pro football circuits," the article began. "The National League presents Tommygun Thompson and Steve Van Buren of the Philadelphia Eagles. The All-

America Conference counters with Automatic Otto Graham and Marion Motley of the Cleveland Browns."

The article drew no conclusions as to which duo was better, but did note that the 7-1-1 Eagles had practically wrapped up their division for the second straight year. The following week, Neale's squad made it official with their fourth shutout of the season, a 17-0 win over Pittsburgh. Pete Pihos had a big game, catching seven passes for 112 yards and a touchdown.

At this point, the Eagles appeared ready to go toe-to-toe with the Western winner, but the Birds stumbled in their next-to-last game of the season. Against a Boston team that was 2-9, the Eagles were hammered, 37-14. A championship, it appeared, was not going to be that easy.

"With a season average of about 42 points per game, we were defeated by about 35 points," remembered Cliff Patton, exaggerating the extent of the defeat a bit. "That was the awakening of our ballclub."

The next week, as the Cardinals were beating the Bears for the Western title, the Eagles concluded the regular season with a 45-21 victory over Detroit. Jack Ferrante had the best day of his career, catching seven passes for 184 yards and three touchdowns. The Eagles offense had proved to be explosive, scoring 50 touchdowns in 12 games, a franchise record that still stands, despite today's 16-game schedule. Individually, Thompson had completed 57 percent of his passes, throwing 25 touchdowns and only 11 interceptions. Van Buren had led the league in rushing with 945 yards (Trippi, with 690, was second), while Bosh Pritchard had added 517 more. Pihos and Ferrante had combined for 18 touchdown receptions. Cliff Patton converted all 50 extra points and kicked eight field goals. And the defense had given up only 156 points, second to the Bears.

But the embarrassing loss to the Yankees, as well as the 21-14 opening-week defeat by the Cardinals, left the Eagles as slight underdogs for the championship game, scheduled for Dec. 19 in Shibe Park. On Dec. 18, the Associated Press, noting that only the Bears had been able to win back-to-back NFL titles, said the Cardinals were favored by 3 1/2 points.

Both coaches were confident that they could prevent a repeat of last year's defensive lapses: Jimmy Conzelman expected the Cardinals to be able to stop Tommy Thompson, and Greasy Neale told the Associated Press that the Cardinals would find it "mighty hard" to trample the middle of his line again.

"The difference," the Associated Press concluded, "in this year's game may ride on the improved reserve strength the Eagles can muster on the line and on a top flight performance by Steve Van Buren."

They continued: "There really is little to choose between the teams. League statistics reveal two evenly matched squads in almost every department of the game. The breaks and weather possibly may determine the final outcome.

"The weatherman predicts either rain or snow or a mixture of both."

*****

On Dec. 19, the city of Philadelphia had a blizzard and an NFL championship game.

The city awoke that Sunday to a driving snowstorm. In suburban Pennfield, where he lived with his wife, Steve Van Buren woke up, looked outside, and went back to bed, assuming the game was canceled. An hour later, Van Buren decided he better go to Shibe Park, just in case. He made his usual trek, taking the trolley, then the Broad Street Subway, then walking eight blocks to the stadium. When he got there, he discovered that there was going to be a game after all.

It's not quite clear why the two teams ended up playing that day. Cancellations were not unthinkable in those days; in years past, games had even been *rained* out. The Cardinals have always said that they didn't want to play. Some of the Eagles have said that they weren't eager to play, but deferred to the wishes of the Cardinals, whom they were told had voted to play. Some accounts say both teams consented to play eagerly; others suggest that it was all the doing of the commissioner, Bert Bell. Regardless, football was played.

The first task of the players was to clear the tarpaulin off the field.

The ground crew alone couldn't do it, so the players were asked to help. Eagles end Dick Humbert recalled:

"They got the Cardinals out, all the football team, and they got all of us out before we went out and warmed up. And what had happened was we started rolling the tarp off, and as you can imagine, every time you rolled it a yard or two, you picked up snow and it got bigger and bigger. Just like a snowball rolling out . . . Well, we got rolling it off and, man, you just couldn't roll it. We were huffing and shoving it.

"My friends who were at the game said it was the most beautiful sight you ever saw. We had the Eagles down there with their silver and gray uniforms on, and they had the Cardinals out there in their Cardinal and white, and then they had the snow. . . . And we were all down in there with our shoulders on this big tarp, moving it. And we moved it almost off the field. Well, we got it off the sidelines."

The best efforts of the two teams had made it possible for the game to be played, though the field was again covered with snow by the time the game started. Yard markers were not visible. Bert Bell ruled that while the 10-yard chain would be used, there would be no measuring; referee Ron Gibbs was to be the final judge of all first downs. The sidelines were marked with ropes tied to stakes. Three alternate officials, in addition to the regular five, were utilized.

The stands, meanwhile, were filling up as fans fought their way through the storm to get to Shibe Park. A total of 28,864 ultimately showed up. A half-hour after its scheduled start, the 1948 championship game got under way.

The Cardinals received the opening kickoff and didn't get anywhere. Ray Mallouf punted and the Eagles took over at the 35. The snow had not let up, but the Eagles decided to try a special pass play, designed by Allie Sherman, who had become the player-coach of the Paterson Panthers in the American Association. Dick Humbert was to head up field and turn in, drawing the attention of Cardinals defensive back Marshall Goldberg. Then Jack Ferrante was to head straight down field, and Tommy Thompson was to hit him.

"Thompson," wrote Louis Effrat of the New York Times, "fired a long pass to Jack Ferrante who, though covered by two defenders, caught the ball on the Cardinal 20. His face in the snow when he fell, Ferrante was the first to untrack himself, and while the two Chicagoans sprawled in the snow, he picked himself up and mushed into the end zone."

It looked as if the Eagles had drawn first blood, but the play was called back. Lost in the snow was a white penalty flag; the call was offsides. Ferrante marched back up the field and demanded to know who was offside. The official, Charlie Berry, told him: "You."

"Oh man, was I mad at that," recounted Ferrante. "Charlie Berry . . . he was the official. He said I was offside. But I doubt very much I was offside because, playing in the snow, where could you line up? I lined up next to where the tackle lined up and we were lined up on sort of an angle. There was no line; you couldn't see where were you were lining up. . . . I was so mad because we had practiced that play for weeks."

Whether or not Ferrante was offsides, that play was about it for the passing offense that day. Seven passes were completed that day, but only four of them were caught by receivers on the same team as the quarterback. Net passing yardage for the game was 42.

What followed, for most of the first three quarters, was a seesaw battle up and down the field. The Cardinals never got closer than the 30-yard line. They reached that spot late in the first quarter and tried a field goal, which the usually accurate Pat Harder missed. From that point on, the Cardinals did not come close to scoring.

The Eagles were able to move the ball somewhat better. In the second quarter, the Eagles recovered a fumble by Elmer Angsman on the Chicago 21. The Cardinals, however, got the ball back as Red Cochran picked off a Tommy Thompson pass. A few plays later, Ray Mallouf punted and Eagles defensive back Pat McHugh returned the ball to the 21. The Eagles got to the 8, but were unable to get into the end zone. Cliff Patton then missed a field goal. At the half, it was a scoreless tie.

It became clear that a big break would be needed to win the game. At the start of the second half, the Cardinals got one as Steve Van Buren fumbled the ball at mid-field. The Cardinals got to the 31 and were stymied. Later in the third quarter, a hand-off from Ray Mallouf to

Elmer Angsman was botched, and Bucko Kilroy recovered at the 17. The Eagles had their chance.

"It wasn't Ray Mallouf's fault," Cardinals coach Jimmy Conzelman said afterward. "It wasn't anybody's fault. It was a little mix-up in a hand-off."

On their first play, Eagles halfback Bosh Pritchard carried to the 11. On the next play, the first play of the final quarter, Joe Muha gained three yards. Thompson followed with a three-yard gain that gave the Eagles a first down. The Eagles then turned to Steve Van Buren. He took the ball, headed behind Al Wistert, and crashed into the end zone. Cliff Patton converted the extra point and the Eagles had a 7-0 lead.

From then on, it was Tommy Thompson's show. Late in the fourth quarter, when the Cardinals had the Eagles backed up to the 7 and were eagerly anticipating another shot at the end zone, Thompson smashed 18 yards on a quarterback sneak. After that, he gave the ball to Pritchard and Van Buren and let them eat up the clock.

The Cardinals finally stopped the Eagles and got the ball back, but lost it again quickly as defensive back Ernie Steele picked off a pass by backup quarterback Charley Eikenberg. The Eagles then ran out the clock as Thompson–carrying the ball three times himself–directed his team to the Cardinal 2, where the game ended. By then, Cliff Patton recalled, there was 8 inches of fresh snow on the ground.

"We knew a break would win the game," Conzelman said. "The Eagles got it and capitalized. They outplayed us and the better team on the field won."

Thompson, Van Buren, and Pritchard had combined to carry the ball 53 times for 215 yards. In comparison, the Cardinals had gained only 96 yards on the ground, with the trio of Charley Trippi, Pat Harder, and Elmer Angsman being held to about 30 yards each. The Eagles' defensive front had held.

Greasy Neale was unstinting in his praise of Tommy Thompson, who had run for 50 yards himself. Thompson, "was the key," Neale said. "He called almost every play and called them right." Thompson, meanwhile, joked that he was going to become a running back next year. "That Steve Van Buren can't go on forever."

The 1948 championship game remains the only NFL title game ever played in a blizzard. Many of the Cardinals were bitter that they were dethroned under such abominable conditions.

"The game should never have been played," recalled Marshall Goldberg. "The field was in no condition to play. There were no sidelines, no end lines; the goal lines were completely obliterated. And, it was just a miserable, such a miserable day that there was no possible way that a decent football game could be played, especially a championship game."

But the Eagles, who almost to a man say they would have beaten the Cardinals in the 1947 title game if the footing at Comiskey Park had been better, felt that they had earned every inch of their victory. This was more than just another free dinner at Bookbinder's; this was their destiny, the NFL championship.

"I know when the day came to play the championship game in '48 and it was snowing like a bitch, Greasy called all of us in the dressing room and almost cried," recalled back Jim Parmer. "We had a chance to put the game off until the next week but we were getting pretty close to Christmas and the players voted to play it that day. And Greasy almost had a fit. He said, 'You dumb son-of-a-bitches, you'll lose this ballgame in this snow' and just raised hell with us, but we went ahead and played it. And we won it."

There's a classic photograph of the team in the locker room after the game. Neale and Van Buren are in the center of the locker room, with Van Buren holding the game ball. Van Buren has a slight grin, and Al Wistert is at Van Buren's side, beaming with pride. The trio are surrounded by a sea of faces, all grinning a grin of glory. Neale looks like the proudest father in the world.

"The experience and the memories of, and the honor, of playing on a world championship football team," recalled Parmer, "is something that I, if I thought all day long, I couldn't describe it. It's something that . . . means more to you than you would be able to put in words."

5

THE BUSINESS & THE BROWNS

****

Three days before the NFL and AAFC played their respective 1948 title games, Eagles owner Alexis Thompson threw the NFL for a loop.

With the annual league meetings set to begin in a few days, he announced that he was going to "feel out" his fellow owners about some kind of peace initiative toward the AAFC. He made it clear that this gesture was not out of altruism or a desire to see how his Eagles would do against the Browns. This move came about because Thompson couldn't stand to lose any more money.

"I'd like to make some 'sense and cents' out of this muddled pro-football business," Thompson was quoted as saying by the Associated Press.

"Please understand, I'm not the kind that changes his mind on this subject every 24 hours. I'm 100 percent in back of any policy the league decides on but I'd be a fool if I didn't try and resolve a situation for which most of us are losing money," the steel tycoon added.

Thompson said that his team, on the verge of winning the championship, was going to "lose close to $32,000." His suggestion: a single draft for both leagues, something that would cut down on the bidding war for players.

"I tried last year," he said, "but nobody would even second my motion for a discussion of the problem."

NFL commissioner Bert Bell was not enthralled with Thompson's ideas.

"The National Football League is satisfied with its operation this year in view of the general falling off of the entertainment business," Bell told the Associated Press.

But Thompson had statistical evidence on his side. Attendance figures released that day showed a decline for the year in both leagues. When the AAFC owners convened on the 17th for their annual meeting, talk of a merger was in the air. Admiral Jonas Ingram, commissioner of the AAFC, said he anticipated peace with the NFL within 30 days. There was even talk that a game between the winners of the two championship games might be arranged. The speculation almost eclipsed the league title games themselves.

******

By December 1948, it was clear that some of the franchises in the AAFC had serious problems. Some, basically, had never gotten off the ground. But the AAFC had two unqualified successes. One was the San Francisco 49ers, which had done everything right except win the league title. The other was the Cleveland Browns. They had done everything right.

Looking back at the AAFC, it's easy to remember those two teams, the survivors, and forget the rest of the league. But the league did make a run at the big time and, for a few years, offered decent football in a number of cities. The Los Angeles, New York, and Buffalo teams enjoyed some success, at least spurts of success, and all fielded interesting teams. The Yankees showcased backs Orban "Spec" Sanders, who had three stellar seasons before wrecking his knee in 1949, and Claude "Buddy" Young, a 5-foot-4 speedster, while the Los Angeles Dons featured Glenn Dobbs in the backfield. Buffalo's fine offense was built around halfback Chet Mutryn and end Al Baldwin.

The AAFC also had some true duds. The Miami Seahawks, professional football's first foray into the Deep South, lost 11 of their 14 games in 1946. They apparently lost large amounts of money as well: The AAFC revoked their franchise at the end of the season for violating the league's debt clause. Except for former LSU halfback William A. "Dub" Jones, who became a star with the Browns, almost all of their players then vanished into obscurity.

The Chicago franchise managed to make it through all four seasons, but struggled mightily. Competing with the Cardinals and Bears, they came in a distant third when it came to the loyalty of Chicagoans. They changed executives and coaches regularly. Owner Jack Keeshin began the 1946 season with Dick Hanley as coach and ended it with Pat Boland, with players Bob Dove, Ned Mathews, and Willie Wilkin serving as co-coaches for five games in the middle. When the 1947 season began, AAFC commissioner Jim Crowley had become both general manager and coach. During the season, he fired himself as coach and put Hamp Pool in that position.

The Rockets did have some marquee talent: Notre Dame Heisman Trophy winner Angelo Bertelli played for them, as did a pair of renowned Indiana backs, Bob "Hunchy" Hoernschemeyer and Billy Hillenbrand. They also featured Elroy "Crazy Legs" Hirsch, a halfback from the University of Wisconsin who would eventually become one of pro football's greatest receivers. But the team was terrible.

"We were a pretty poor team. There weren't a lot of good memories," recalled Hirsch. "We were 1-13 the last two years (1947 and 1948). So, it wasn't very much fun playing.

"We'd play in Soldier Field which, of course, was a huge stadium, is a huge stadium, and we'd have only a couple thousand people in there. You know you couldn't find them. Mostly friends and parents and wives and that sort of thing."

"It was a new league, and no one was there, that's all," recalled Bertelli, who spent two of his three years in pro football with the Rockets.

But, while some of the AAFC's teams struggled, two solid franchises emerged, the San Francisco 49ers and the Cleveland Browns.

The 49ers were owned by Tony Morabito, who had been rejected in 1944 when he applied to the NFL for a franchise, and coached by Lawrence "Buck" Shaw. They played in Kezar Stadium and had a solid fan base from day one. On the field, their leaders were two former backfield mates from Clark Shaughnessy's Stanford teams: captain Norm Standlee, a fullback and linebacker, and Frankie Albert, a small but slippery quarterback. Albert was a real crowd-pleaser.

"He was a field general, a left-hander, was very adept at running the ball, a great ball-handler, and he was a very accurate passer," recalled end Gordy Soltau of Albert. "He wasn't a long deep thrower like some of the boys–like (Bob) Waterfield and (Norm) Van Brocklin, that style–but he could get out it there where he had to. And he was extremely competitive and very knowledgeable, and he was like a coach on the field."

******

In 1946, the 49ers finished second to Cleveland with a 9-5 mark, but did hand the Browns one of their two defeats. In 1947, the 49ers lost to the Browns twice and finished second in the West with a 8-4-2 mark. Cleveland's Otto Graham threw a total of five touchdown passes in the two victories.

That season, Cleveland was even more imposing than it had been in 1946, losing only to the Los Angeles Dons. On Nov. 23, playing before the second-largest crowd to see a pro game in New York since the days of Red Grange, Otto Graham brought Cleveland back from a 28-0 halftime deficit to tie the Yankees, 28-28. "Graham established a conference passing record by gaining 325 yards on 15 completions in 28 attempts," the Associated Press said.

Cleveland won their other 12 regular-season games by such scores as 55-7, 42-0, and 37-14. In the title game Dec. 14 before 60,103 in New York, the Browns beat the Yankees, 14-3. Two long runs by Marion Motley set up touchdowns by Otto Graham and former Bears halfback Edgar "Special Delivery" Jones.

"Spec Sanders of the Yankees, billed as the game's greatest player, was a complete flop, perhaps due to his bad ankle," wrote the

International News Service. "He picked up a mere 40 yards from scrimmage and failed to score a touchdown for the first time this year.

"Big Marion Motley and Otto Graham starred for Cleveland. Motley leveled off the New York linemen like a steamroller."

In 1948, San Francisco seemed ready to challenge the Browns juggernaut. All-Pro Riley Matheson joined the 49ers from the NFL's Rams, teaming with former Eagle Bruno Banducci, John Woudenberg, and Visco Grgich to give the squad one of the best lines in pro football. (Grgich, a native of Yugoslavia, was famous for breaking down the locker room door at Kezar Stadium before the start of each game.)

Their other significant addition was Fletcher Joseph Perry, an unheralded 21-year-old back from Compton Junior College and the Alameda Naval Air Station team. On his first play with the 49ers, he ran 58 yards for a touchdown. "Joe the Jet" became San Francisco's first black star and joined Marion Motley, Bill Willis, Horace Gillom and Buddy Young in the AAFC's growing galaxy of African-American heroes.

The 49ers had a spectacular offense in 1948. They had two distinct backfields: Their first-string unit of Albert, Perry, Johnny "Strike" Strzykalski, and Len Eshmont averaged more than 6 yards a carry and scored 23 touchdowns, while their second-string unit of Bev Wallace, Verl Lillywhite, Forrest Hall, and Standlee averaged more than 7 yards a carry and scored eight touchdowns. Alyn Beals, whom Strzykalski described as "the best end in pro football that I played with or against," caught a league-leading 14 touchdown passes. The team scored 69 touchdowns, a total that would still be pretty impressive in today's NFL.

The 49ers beat Buffalo, 35-14, in their opener, and were not held below 35 points until the sixth game of the year, when they beat Chicago, 31-14. The following week, they pounced on Baltimore, 56-14. In Week 10, they beat Chicago, 44-21, to run their record to 10-0. The only problem for the 49ers at that point was that Paul Brown's amazing Browns also were unbeaten.

*****

It is sometimes hard to separate the myths surrounding Paul Brown and his AAFC juggernaut from the facts. His career has become such a blur that all of his coaching innovations seem to have come about all at once. The only one of his innovations that is fixed in time is the one that failed, his experiment with radio transmitters for the quarterback's helmet in 1956. It's also likely that he is credited with some things that were actually originated by less-famous coaches; for instance, some historians suggest that it was probably Clark Shaughnessy, not Brown, who came up with the playbook. Still, it is clear that Brown approached coaching differently than other people did.

Brown was the ultimate organization man. He believed that a winning team needed not only a great coach, but also a solid foundation, one that dug up great players and then molded them into a smoothly functioning team. Everything he did was designed to create a structure that was conducive to winning.

"He was probably as well-organized as anybody who's ever coached in the history of football," Otto Graham recalled. "I've always said that there were other coaches who knew as much football as he knew, but none of them were as well-organized as he was. . . . When you put it all together, he's probably the best coach ever to coach the game, and, of course, his record proves it."

"He left nothing to chance," guard Lindell L. Houston, who played for Brown in high school, college, and the pros, told the Massillon Independent after Brown died in August 1991. "He was detail-oriented and wouldn't assume anything."

Brown had a system for everything and he expected everyone to learn it. Some aspects of his system were new and different–for instance, he called the plays instead of the quarterback–but he felt compelled to teach his players everything, even things that one could be reasonably sure that they already knew. There are even stories that he began his annual introductory talk at training camp with, "Gentlemen, this is a football." That tale may be exaggerated, but, regardless, Paul Brown's troops were expected to pay absolute attention to his teachings.

"There was no great mysteries attached to our success," Brown said in his autobiography. "We were meticulous in all our preparations and we even practiced how to practice."

And, Brown took the game home with him. He expected everyone in the organization to be thinking about football full time during the season, and he demanded that his coaching staff and scouts work year-round. "There was no dignity, I felt, in having a man coach our offensive line for six months and then sell automobiles for six months," Brown said at one point. He preferred they spend their "free" months looking at film.

"He would not only prepare a team with game films, but he took them and analyzed them at the end of the season," recalled tackle Lou Groza.

"He assigned them to coaches to grade their positions . . . How many blocks you attempt, how many you made, how many you missed. Then they also would grade you on your techniques. In other words, they broke down the block into four parts: stance, approach, contact, and follow-through. They'd tell you what part of your blocking was the weakest."

He intruded upon his players in ways that other coaches never had. He used IQ and psychological tests in scouting his players, and was the first to use a stopwatch to see how fast they were. Brown even had a rule, known as the Tuesday Rule, in which he asked his players to refrain from having sex from Wednesday on in order to preserve their energy for Sunday's games. (No, this rule was not enforced.)

Brown expected civility and decency from his players. His team would attend a movie together the night before a game, and he emphasized the importance of table manners in his annual introductory talk at training camp. "There have been people who failed to make this team simply because they were obnoxious to eat with," he would say. His players were also expected to be tolerant: Both Marion Motley and Bill Willis have said that it was clear that newcomers to the Browns were told that they had accept playing with blacks or else. The duo had to put up with taunts and cheap shots from their foes, but not from their teammates.

"When Paul signed us, there were a few (Browns) who weren't too happy," Motley told writer Ray Didinger in 1995. "Paul addressed that at the first meeting. He said, 'If you can't get along with your teammates, you won't be here.' He didn't have to spell it out, everyone knew what he meant."

This was a team of dignity, and players who failed to live up to Brown's standards were replaced. In 1946, captain Jim Daniell was released two days before the championship game after an arrest for intoxication. Though the charges were later dropped, Daniell's career with the Browns was over.

"You've got to give Paul Brown the credit," said Graham. "In any business, you've got to surround yourself with high-class people, people who are willing to work hard, put forth extra effort, you know–they aren't yes men, but when you're told this is the way we're gonna do it, they break their butts to get it done. That's the kind of people he hired.

"He hired high-class players too, generally speaking. If he found one that was running around, getting in all kinds of trouble, he'd get rid of them. Because he would tell us in our very first meeting every year, if you go into a bar and start getting drunk and raising hell, it's not Joe Blow that's getting drunk, it's the Cleveland Browns getting drunk. We don't want that kind of reputation, period, and won't tolerate it. The guys didn't smoke or drink ever in front of Paul Brown. We could never go into the lobby of a hotel with T shirts on; you had to wear a coat and tie. He said he wanted us to be known as just like his college team was at Ohio State, a high-class college team. And we were."

"Paul would not sign a player unless he was a class act," recalled Weldon G. Humble, a guard for whom Brown traded five players to Buffalo in 1947.

Brown's teams were not the most physical teams in the sport; they didn't wear out opponents the way that, say, the Chicago Bears did. But Brown, like Greasy Neale, insisted on stop-on-a-dime execution, and he demanded that his players not only practice but also intently study the game. Newcomers who didn't appreciate the value of blackboard study, who didn't think they had anything to learn from him, were quickly shown the door. Again, it's impossible to determine how much of Brown's approach to the game was new, but it is clear that he put more emphasis on organization than anyone ever had. He approached football as if he were working on a doctoral degree in it and left his mark on everyone who played for him.

"I always had a great admiration for Paul Brown," said end-kicker Gordy Soltau, who was in Cleveland's camp as a rookie in 1950 before being traded to San Francisco, where he played nine seasons. "In the two weeks that I spent with him, I learned more about playing football and playing your position and understanding . . . many of the subtleties of the game that I never had the opportunity to learn prior to that. . . . It certainly was helpful the rest of my career."

It helped, of course, that Brown was an excellent judge of talent. He was able to trade a player like Soltau because he already had Dante Lavelli and Mac Speedie at end, and Lou Groza doing the kicking. All three were All-Pros.

The end combination was a dynamic one. Speedie had overcome a crippling childhood bone ailment that struck when he was 6–his left leg was shorter and narrower than his right one, and he wore a leg brace for a considerable time–to become a fine amateur boxer, a world-class hurdler at the University of Utah, and a first lieutenant in the Army. Speedie's childhood troubles were pretty much of a secret until 1949, when his mother, Nell Speedie, decided to let everyone know what her son had overcome. (One of the most-repeated anecdotes at the time: Nell had to rush home one day because young Mac was on the roof of their house, showing his friends that his leg brace didn't stop him from climbing.) In the AAFC, Speedie's forte was big plays; he caught the first touchdown pass in league history and went on to average almost 17 yards per reception from 1946 to 1949.

Lavelli had been a halfback on Brown's 1942 national championship team at Ohio State before entering the Army. Once converted to end, he was so sure-handed that he acquired the nickname "Glue Fingers." A terrific competitor, he took double coverage from the defense to be a compliment. "I figure," Lavelli told writer Mort Berry in 1950, "you are not good if one man can cover you. You are moving and the defensive back is standing still." In today's terms, one would describe Speedie as the deep threat and Lavelli as the possession receiver.

"Mac Speedie had more natural ability than Dante did, but Dante had the greatest pair of hands I've ever seen. He'd be surrounded by guys, and I'd throw the ball at his voice because I knew nine out of 10 times he'd come down with it. He'd fight, bite, kick to get the ball. He was that kind of guy," recalled Otto Graham. "Mac Speedie did not have glue fingers. He had great speed and so forth, but he did not have glue fingers. He didn't fight for the ball the way that Dante would."

Quiet and sensible Lou Groza was the place-kicker, a job he would hold for 21 seasons. Though his reputation for incredible accuracy in clutch situations would not develop for a few years (the Browns simply didn't have many close games in their early years), he did kick a ton of extra points and more than his share of field goals during the team's AAFC years. Starting in 1947, the Browns also had an exceptional punter, Horace Gillom, another of Brown's favorites from his Massillon High days. After getting some seasoning at the University of Nevada in 1946, Gillom became the Browns' punter and a useful end, particularly on defense. "Gillom punts the ball so high and far," quipped writer Mort Berry, "a fast eater could consume two hot dogs and three bottles of pop before it comes down." Paul Brown liked to call Gillom the best punter in the history of pro football.

Groza also became a starter on the line in 1948. Tackle Lou Rymkus, a former Redskin from Notre Dame, was the first star on the front wall but there were other stalwarts as well: Center-linebacker Frank "Gunner" Gatski, guards Weldon G. Humble, Ed Ulinski and Lin Houston, defensive end George Young, and linebackers Lou Saban and Tony Adamle. Most notable of all was "Deacon" Bill Willis, a small but lightning-quick guard.

Willis played at just over 200 pounds but made up for it with his speed–writer Robert Treat referred to it as "pantherine leg-spring." When Willis came to the Browns in August 1946 and tried out on defense at middle guard, he was getting to the quarterback so quickly that the center insisted Willis had to be, *just had to be*, offside. Brown and assistant

Blanton Collier watched him carefully and realized that the center was wrong. They also realized that Willis had the makings of a superstar.

Willis excelled at middle guard, going over and around much larger players. George Allen later pronounced him the best middle guard ever, and the experts in Rick Korch's *The Truly Great,* at a loss at what position to rank him, named him the second-best nose tackle. Korch quoted Bears great Clyde "Bulldog" Turner as saying, "About the first guy that ever convinced me that I couldn't handle anybody I ever met was Bill Willis."

As good as Willis and company were, the true stars of the Browns were two of their backs, Otto Graham and Marion Motley. Even with Paul Brown calling the plays, Graham was the team's unquestioned leader on the field. For his part, Graham attributed a good part of his success to the players around him.

"I happened to have good protection. I could never throw the ball lying flat on my back. So I had to have protection," he said. "I also had to have receivers who get open. And then I had to throw the football. All three parts are important."

Graham could certainly throw the ball. "Automatic Otto" became known as a precise passer, particularly when it came to sideline routes. The former Northwestern University music student from Waukegan, Ill., was also a stellar athlete (he briefly played professional basketball) capable of making a big play on defense or running with the ball. Paul Brown called him the best quarterback of all time, and others have ranked Graham right up there as well.

"Graham didn't have to throw as much as some of the more recent quarterbacking stars," wrote George Allen in *Pro Football's 100 Greatest Players,* "but he gained a lot of yardage with the throws he did make. He was accurate and intelligent with his passes and difficult to intercept. His ball-handling was good, and he made very few mistakes."

Above all, Graham was a winner. According to the win-lost percentages in *The Pro Football Chronicle,* Graham's teams won almost 85 percent of their games. Recent quarterbacks like John Elway and Dan Marino may have won more games, but neither could match Graham's winning percentage. It was Graham's win-lost record that led Paul Brown to speak glowingly of him every chance he got. "Otto was my greatest player because he played the most important position. He was the crux of how we got to things," he was quoted as saying by writer Mickey Herskowitz. At other times, Brown simply called him "the greatest player in the game's history."

If Brown was the team's navigator and Graham its pilot, then Marion Motley was its bombardier. Motley, unfortunately, has been relegated to the status of cult hero: He has never become a hero of the popular imagination in the way that, say, Joe DiMaggio or Willie Mays have. When he died in June 1999, many newspapers gave his obituary only a few paragraphs. But those who saw Motley and played with him speak of him only in the most reverent of terms.

Motley was 26 when he entered the league as a 238-pound fullback-linebacker, but from day one, he was a dominating figure. In his first season, Motley averaged 8.2 yards per carry, one of the best averages of all time.

Motley's specialty was a trap play through the center of the line. "If there is someone in front of you," Paul Brown told him, "just run in one end of him and out the other." He was also a potent weapon on the screen pass. Both plays kept their foes from concentrating too much on stopping Graham and his dynamic ends.

In 1947, Motley averaged 6.0 yards per carry in rushing for 889 yards and also accumulated 322 yards as a kick returner. 1948 was his best year: He carried 157 times for an AAFC-leading 964 yards, adding 192 yards on pass receptions and 337 on kick returns. In the four AAFC championship games, he carried the ball 48 times for 415 yards and five touchdowns.

Statistics tell only a small part of the story. Motley didn't actually carry the ball much; in 1948, he averaged just over 11 carries per game (Steve Van Buren had 16.75 per game that year) and that was the most that Motley ever ran the ball. The rest of the time, Motley was a hellacious blocker, as well as a first-rate linebacker. He also made a contribution to the sport's strategy: Motley and Otto Graham inadvertently invented the draw play one game when Graham, facing an onslaught of pass rushers deep in the backfield, handed the ball to his blocking back.

In *The New Thinking Man's Guide to Pro Football,* Paul Zimmerman presented his case for Motley as the greatest football player of all time, offering supporting evidence from a slew of former coaches and players, including former Browns assistants Blanton Collier and Weeb Ewbank. Zimmerman cited Motley's all around-play. "He was dynamic and terrifying, but it was his pass blocking that really lifted him into a different dimension," he wrote. "Motley's style was a numbing, paralyzing head-and-shoulders shot that would lift defensive ends and tackles and dump them on their behind."

Graham has frequently called Motley the best fullback ever, and Bill Willis has described him as a great all-around player, praising his play at linebacker in their goal-line defense. Many of those who played against Motley also were in awe of him: "Marion Motley not only helped break the color barrier in professional football, he broke a few opponents' helmets with his punishing runs and devastating blocks," Tom Landry wrote in his autobiography.

*****

With Graham perfecting the precision passing game and Motley keeping the defenses honest, the Browns had an offense that could rival San Francisco's, even though they didn't score quite as frequently. On defense, however, the Browns were clearly superior to the 49ers. In their first nine games in 1948, the Browns did not allow an opponent to score more than 17 points. On Nov. 14, before 82,768 fans in Cleveland, the 10-0 49ers and 9-0 Browns collided, and defense carried the day.

"The mighty Cleveland Browns, unaccustomed to sharing leadership with anybody, finally booted the San Francisco 49ers out of co-partnership atop the All-America Conference pro football standings yesterday," the Associated Press said. The score was 14-7 and the game was a rugged one, with Mac Speedie suffering a separated shoulder.

Still, the 49ers were not finished yet. They outlasted Brooklyn, 63-40, to put themselves at 11-1 for the rematch with the Browns. The Browns, meanwhile, had to play three road games on two coasts in eight days. On Nov. 21, they got a superlative game from Motley–a 78-

yard touchdown reception and 75 yards rushing–to beat the pesky Yankees, 34-21. Four days later, the Los Angeles Dons stayed close to the Browns until the third quarter before Cleveland prevailed, 31-14. Graham injured a knee against the Dons, giving him only three days to heal before the Browns-49ers rematch in San Francisco. Dante Lavelli, Mac Speedie and Tommy James were also banged up.

But Graham played, and once again the 49ers fell painfully short. San Francisco jumped out to a 21-10 lead, but Graham then took over, throwing touchdown passes to Marion Motley, Dub Jones, and Special Delivery Jones in an eight-minute span to give the Browns a 31-28 victory at Kezar Stadium. The win guaranteed that the Browns would represent the AAFC's West in the championship game for the third straight year, and that San Francisco, unbeaten against the league's other six teams, would sit home.

"The only difference between us," 49ers lineman Visco Grgich told writer Dave Newhouse in 1983, "was that they had so highly developed the sideline pass pattern to Dante Lavelli and Mac Speedie. We'd hold them, it would be third-and-10, and Otto Graham would complete that darn sideline pass for a first down."

In the last week of the season, the Browns beat Brooklyn, 31-21, to conclude a 14-0 regular season. The championship game against Buffalo was almost anti-climactic. The Browns were 13-point favorites over the 7-7 Bills and had decisively beaten them twice during the season.

Cleveland's defense did most of the work in the title game, setting up touchdowns in each of the first three quarters. An interception by back Tommy James led to Cleveland's first score of the game, a 3-yard run by Special Delivery Jones. The second touchdown came on a fumble recovery and 18-yard run by end George Young. In the third quarter, another interception led to Special Delivery Jones' second touchdown of the day, this one coming on a 9-yard pass from Otto Graham.

Marion Motley then went to work, scoring on runs of 29, 31, and 5 yards as the Browns built a 42-7 lead before Cleveland linebacker Lou Saban concluded the scoring by running an interception back for a touchdown. It was a dominating performance; Motley led the way with 133 yards rushing on 14 carries, while Graham completed 11 of

24 passes for 118 yards. Buffalo quarterbacks George Ratterman and Jim Still were intercepted five times.

After the game, Brown told the Associated Press that his squad was "the greatest team I've ever coached" and had special individual praise for Motley. "That Motley, he really was a snoot full, wasn't he? He's the greatest fullback in history and that includes Bronko Nagurski," Brown proclaimed.

The Associated Press reported that bad weather had cut the crowd to 22,981, making the players' shares only $594.18, but Brown said his team was "fired to the limit" by the chance to complete a season undefeated.

"They were as anxious as a kid about to drive his dad's car for the first time," he said.

Then, Brown issued a challenge. He said he was willing to take on the NFL champion Eagles "any time, any place."

With talks between the owners scheduled for the day after the game, it seemed entirely possible that such a matchup could be played very soon.

******

The peace talks quickly fizzled. The AAFC wanted to keep as many of its franchises alive as possible, but the NFL's hard-line owners, particularly George Preston Marshall of the Washington Redskins, wanted peace only if it reduced competition, not enhanced it.

On Dec. 17, AAFC commissioner Jonas Ingram had talked about a peace where all but one (Chicago) of the AAFC teams would survive. Four days later, however, it was reported that the fledgling league was trying to merge four of its eight franchises into the NFL–Cleveland, San Francisco, Los Angeles, and Baltimore.

The biggest sticking point was Baltimore. Marshall owned one of the league's two most profitable franchises (the Bears were the other) and didn't want a competing franchise within an hour's drive. "What do we want Baltimore for? We have enough of our own headaches without adding any more," Marshall told The Associated Press..

Cleveland owner Arthur "Mickey" McBride disclosed that the NFL countered with a proposal to retain only his team and San Francisco, two franchises located in cities where the NFL had no teams. The meeting ended with the leagues at an impasse. They had not been able to achieve something as simple as the common draft that Eagles owner Alexis Thompson proposed.

NFL publicist Joseph Labrum read a joint statement: "Representatives of the National Football League and All America Conference concluded a meeting in Philadelphia tonight. . . . The committee terminated the meeting with the expectation that future meetings might provide some formula for a common understanding between both leagues."

For some owners, the impasse was the last straw. On Jan. 5, it was announced that Thompson was selling the Eagles. Nine days later, a group of 100 Philadelphians, referred to as the "100 brothers," bought the team, each paying $2,500 and putting up an additional $500 for operating capital. The leader was James P. Clark, a trucking magnate.

"The purchasing group represents a cross-section of Philadelphia and will dedicate itself to making the Philadelphia Eagles the best community-sponsored football team in America," Clark said in his first statement to the press.

Philadelphia's problems appeared to be over, but there were other trouble spots. On Jan. 21, the NFL's Boston Yankees became the New York Bulldogs. The move was apparently some sort of tax maneuver by owner Ted Collins, whose franchise was a disaster. In addition, the venerable Green Bay Packers were reported to be in dire straits, and the Detroit Lions had been sold in 1948 by Fred Mandel for $40,000 less than he purchased them for in 1940.

The AAFC was in even worse shape. After the failed talks with the NFL, Commissioner Ingram resigned in frustration. The Brooklyn Dodgers, owned by Branch Rickey, merged with the Yankees, bringing the league down to seven teams. Two other teams, Baltimore and Chicago, required infusions of cash from deep-pocketed Ben Lindheimer, whose Los Angeles Dons had been the league's second-best draw in 1947 and whose investors included such Hollywood figures as Louis B.

Mayer and Don Ameche. He had continued to spend liberally even as attendance fell off in 1948.

This was a war of attrition, and not one that was easily won. Today, teams count on other sources of revenue beyond ticket sales, particularly money from television rights. But, owners of sports teams, as well as movie makers and restaurateurs, were terrified of television in the Forties. TV was still such a novelty that people stayed home and watched whatever they could. Televise your games and people would stop coming to the stadium.

Some football owners did flirt with the medium: In 1947, Bears owner George Halas got a local station to pay him $900 per game to televise the Bears' road games. The Eagles, too, recalled guard-kicker Cliff Patton, tried to make some money through local broadcasting. But by 1949, teams were backtracking. According to writer Phil Patton, the Eagles, Giants, and other teams banned television coverage, saying that it was hurting more than helping.

Saving money was not easy for these troubled teams; there was very little fat that could be trimmed. Most teams had small staffs and modest offices–the offices of the NFL's Eagles, for example, were located underneath that of a manufacturer of false teeth. (Longtime team official Jim Gallagher told writer Bill Lyon that staffers would have to shout at each other to be heard over the din.)

At the same time, the ongoing war between the leagues made it impossible for teams to cut players' salaries–a player on a poor team could still jump to one of the sport's healthier teams, as Elroy Hirsch did when he bailed out on the AAFC's Chicago franchise and joined the NFL's Rams for the 1949 season.

Consequently, the bidding wars continued. Both leagues held secret drafts late in the 1948 season to get a head start on bidding for the top players in college football; a Dec. 1, 1948, article by The Associated Press reported that spirited bidding was already under way for college stars Doak Walker, Stan Heath, Johnny Rauch, and Chuck Bednarik. The 1948 pro and college seasons were still going, but teams were already in the hunt for next year's rookie class.

As the 1949 season opened, there were only four stable franchises left in the AAFC, and things got worse as the season progressed. The Dons fielded their worst team and came nowhere near their earlier attendance figures. In Buffalo, the Bills were still drawing well, but Jim Breuil told his fellow AAFC owners that he was pulling out at the end of the year. The AAFC had once more come down to the Browns and the 49ers.

On the field, those two teams again dominated, but this time there was a different twist. Because the AAFC was down to seven teams, the league had scrapped its divisional format and implemented a playoff format involving teams with the four best records. For the first time, Cleveland and San Francisco could play in a championship game.

The AAFC season had a jarring start: In the opener, Cleveland, which had won its last 17 games, was tied by Buffalo, 28-28, in Cleveland. The Browns quickly got back on track, beating Baltimore, New York, Baltimore, and Los Angeles in succession. The 49ers, meanwhile, started off 4-1, scoring 42 points three times in their first five games. On Oct. 9, the teams met in Kezar Stadium.

For the first time since 1946, Buck Shaw's team emerged victorious. The 49ers took a 21-0 lead on two Frankie Albert touchdown passes and a one-yard run by Johnny "Strike" Strzykalski, saw Cleveland close the lead to 35-21 at halftime, and then pulled away, 56-28. The hero was Albert: "The former Stanford magician flipped five scoring aerials in the thrill-a-minute contest," wrote the Associated Press.

"The Cleveland Browns' bubble has burst. In fact, it has exploded," wrote the Associated Press. "After a two-year domination of the All-American Football Conference . . . the Browns finally came apart yesterday, but good."

San Francisco's victory knocked the Browns into second place. Alas, for the 49ers, this triumph was just a prelude to another fall. During a 51-7 victory over Buffalo, the 49ers lost two of their halfbacks, Strzykalski and Ed Carr. Joe Perry picked up some of the load–he ended up leading the AAFC in rushing with 783 yards–but their vaunted running attack started to slip.

The 49ers lost to the Yankees, 24-3, and then lost a rematch to the Browns on Oct. 30. "Revenge was never more toothsome than the retribution possessed by the Cleveland Browns today at the expense of the San Francisco 49ers," said the Associated Press. Otto Graham threw for two touchdowns and scored a third, while Lou Groza booted a key fourth-quarter field goal as the Browns won, 30-28. The win gave the Browns a mark of 6-1-1, and left the 49ers at 6-3. Continued heroics by Perry, Frankie Albert, end Alyn Beals, and guard Visco Grgich enabled the 49ers to win their last three games and finish in second place, one game ahead of their first-round playoff opponents, the Yankees.

The Browns went on to hold their last four opponents to a total of 15 points, in winning three games and tying the fourth, a 7-7 battle with Buffalo, which garnered the league's fourth playoff berth. Cleveland's offensive production was down a bit from 1948, though end Mac Speedie did lead the league in both receptions and yardage, burning a young Yankees defensive back named Tom Landry in one game for 11 receptions and 228 yards. (Landry singled out that afternoon for mention years later in his autobiography.) The vaunted Browns defense held seven of its 12 opponents to a touchdown or less.

After dispatching the Bills and Yankees in first-round playoff games, the Browns and 49ers squared off in the snow Dec. 11 in Cleveland. In the first half, the game was virtually even, with the Browns scoring only on a 2-yard run by Special Delivery Jones. The 49ers kept both Otto Graham and Marion Motley in check, while the Browns stopped Frankie Albert and Joe Perry.

In the second half, however, it was Motley to the rescue for the Browns again. On a trap play, the fullback took the ball 63 yards, giving the Browns a 14-0 lead. The 49ers cut the lead to 14-7 early in the fourth quarter on a 23-yard touchdown pass from Albert to rookie end Paul Salata, but the Browns sealed the win with a 4-yard touchdown run by Dub Jones. The final score was 21-7. Attendance was a mere 22,500.

That game was the last hurrah for the AAFC. Two days before it was played, the two leagues had announced that they would merge and become the National-American Football League effective Dec. 19. The cost for the AAFC was high: Cleveland, San Francisco, and Baltimore were all that was left of their league.

To make matters worse, according to *The Pro Football Chronicle*, Baltimore had to pay the George Preston Marshall and the Washington Redskins $50,000 for so-called territorial rights. The Colts, as the 13th team in the NFL (the reconstituted league abandoned the National-American Football League moniker before it ever went into use), became the NFL's swing team, one that was to play each team in the NFL once in 1950. For a team that had finished its last season in the AAFC at 1-11, these conditions spelled trouble. The franchise had traded slow starvation for what amounted to a death sentence.

Other franchises disappeared. Unaware that their owner had given up on their team and elected to purchase a share of the Browns, the city of Buffalo was stunned when it was excluded from the new league. With a little encouragement from NFL commissioner Bert Bell, residents of Buffalo promptly started collecting season-ticket pledges and raising money in the hopes of demonstrating the viability of the franchise. The NFL declined to hear their pleas. The city would not get another major-league team until Ralph Wilson brought the fourth version of the American Football League to town in 1960. The Dons, Yankees, and Hornets also vanished.

Players from the defunct teams were put into a pool and divided up, though there were some unique arrangements made. In exchange for letting the NFL's Bulldogs move to Yankee Stadium and change their name to the Yankees, the Giants were rewarded with several players from the AAFC's defunct Yankees.

As for San Francisco and Cleveland, the merger didn't significantly alter the landscape for the 49ers. They would be blessed with four fabulous rookies in their first three years in the NFL: tackle Leo Nomellini (1950), receiver-kicker Gordy Soltau (1950), receiver Billy Wilson (1951) and running back Hugh McElhenny (1952). In 1951, after the Colts folded, they would also add quarterback Y.A. Tittle. The team, however, spent much of the 1950s in their old AAFC rut. They were good enough to contend most years but not good enough to win a title. Their first championship would not come until the Bill Walsh-Joe Montana era in the 1980s.

Meanwhile, the Browns got richer. Mickey McBride had given

Buffalo's owner a quarter of his team in return for three of Buffalo's better players, guard Abe Gibron, back Rex Bumgardner, and tackle John Kissell. All would play key roles for the Browns, with Gibron becoming one of the finest guards of his generation. The savvy Browns also grabbed a squeaky-voiced giant named Len Ford from the defunct Dons. The 24-year-old from the University of Michigan would prove to be a holy terror at defensive end. Once again, the Browns had come out ahead of their AAFC brethren when it counted.

6

1949—PLAYING BOTH WAYS

****

After their move from Boston, Ted Collins' New York Bulldogs opened their 1949 season on a Thursday night at the Polo Grounds against the Eagles. In the offseason, Collins had purchased second-year quarterback Bobby Layne from the Bears and hired Charley Ewart from the Eagles as coach. Ewart had spent the previous year working with Greasy Neale, John Kellison, and Larry Cabrelli, serving as backfield coach and general manager.

"He should know what the Eagles are going to do all night long," wrote Al Del Greco, a New Jersey pundit, of Ewart's debut against his old team. "Whether his hirelings can follow his instructions and do something about it is another matter."

Ewart's players did contain the Eagles, holding rushing champion Steve Van Buren to 58 yards on 25 carries. For the game, the Eagles got only a touchdown by Bosh Pritchard, which came after they drove 89 yards on their first possession. Unfortunately for Ewart, his team couldn't move the ball at all. Playing on a muddy field, the Bulldogs managed only one first down as the Eagles won, 7-0. It was one of the more formidable defensive performances in Philadelphia's history.

The following week, the Eagles headed to Detroit. Expectations were high, as Steve Van Buren, beginning his sixth season, needed only 45 yards to break the career rushing record of 3,860 yards set by Green Bay's Clarke Hinkle from 1932 to 1941. Playing on a Monday night, Van Buren got the mark, gaining 135 yards in 33 carries, with a pair of touchdowns. "Man, do those fellows give me good blocking," said a typically humble Van Buren. The Eagles won, 22-14, to boost their record to 2-0.

However, not everybody on the Eagles was happy about the way the season had started. Rookie Chuck Bednarik had not played in the Detroit game and was steamed at Greasy Neale. No ordinary rookie, Bednarik was a former aerial gunner from Bethlehem, Pa., who had gone on to become everybody's all-American at the University of Pennsylvania. Neale's team had landed the 6-foot-3, 230-pound center-linebacker when they had drawn the 1949 bonus pick, the first overall selection in the NFL draft.

"Will Bednarik become as outstanding in the NFL as he was in college?" pondered an article in a 1949 game program. "Probably not. His college coach, George Munger, says no player can be as good as Bednarik is supposed to be. He would have to be a combination of Bronko Nagurski, Red Grange, Pudge Heffelfinger, and Gargantua to be that good."

But Bednarik wasn't competing with the legends of bygone eras quite yet. He was competing with 33-year-old Vic Lindskog at center and 34-year-old Alex Wojciechowicz at linebacker and neither was easy to dislodge. Against Detroit, Neale had played both veterans, while Bednarik sat on the bench for the second straight week.

"I came to Greasy Neale on the way home–we didn't fly, we went by train–and I told him that if he didn't feel I could play on this team, that he should trade me because I want to play," recalled Bednarik.

For whatever reason, Neale took the plea of his heralded rookie to heart and mixed Bednarik, Lindskog, and Wojciechowicz into what was essentially a three-way system. Sometimes, Bednarik recounted, he would play center and Lindskog would sit. Sometimes Bednarik would play linebacker and Wojie would sit. Sometimes both played linebacker, and Joe Muha got a breather. None of them played all the time, and none of them sat all the time, at least as long as they were healthy. This was the first year of unlimited substitution, and Greasy Neale was already taking advantage of his right to mix-and-match his players as he saw fit.

*****

Almost all contemporary discussions about two-way play are incomplete or wrong.

This is the conventional wisdom on the subject: In the past, football's iron men were on the field for 98.9 percent of a 60-minute game, and today they specialize, doing only one very specific task while spending much of the game on the bench. Chuck Bednarik's career is usually treated as the dividing point. In 1960, he played both ways at age 35, and after that, except for the occasional wide receiver-defensive backs like Roy Green, Charles Woodson and Deion Sanders, everybody played either offense or defense. And Sanders, Woodson and Green weren't "real" two-way players, since they didn't play on the line, where the roughest action is.

"I'm the last guy who did it both ways and, like I say, I did it at age 35," recounted Bednarik. "You look at these kids today: After three plays, you see the way they suck and huff and they puff. They're too big, they're too heavy, they're too fat. That's why they cannot do it. . . . It's impossible for an athlete to weigh 280, 290, 300 and play both ways. IMPOSSIBLE!"

Maybe so, but the history of football's conversion from a sport where just about everybody played all the time to one where everybody specializes has become hopelessly oversimplified. There is no precise point in history where the ideal of the 60-minute man was discarded.

In 1948, the year before Bednarik turned professional, a number of the sport's stars are listed by *The Football Encyclopedia* as having played on only one side of the ball. Among them: Sammy Baugh, Sid Luckman, Tommy Thompson, Frank Reagan, Bones Taylor, Marshall Goldberg, Alyn Beals, Frankie Albert, Lou Saban, Dante Lavelli, and Mac Speedie. All had been two-way players at one time, but, for a variety of reasons, were now playing either offense or defense but not both.

In 1961, the year after Bednarik's legendary two-way performance in the NFL championship game, more than two dozen players are listed as having played both on offense and defense, including a number of linemen. None of these men were players of the caliber of Bednarik; the best known are halfback-defensive backs Pat Fischer of the Cardinals and Abe Woodson of the 49ers. It's likely that none of them played extensively on offense and defense in any one game. Yet, they did have the skills and background to play both on offense and defense.

These listings may not be entirely complete or precisely accurate, but they do suggest that the transition from two-way players to one-way players was not a smooth one. The process was one of evolution, one that took into account changes in college play, in the game's rules, and in its strategy. Of the factors that led to this change, probably the most important occurred before Bednarik ever played a down of professional football. That was on Jan. 20, 1949, when the NFL decided to permit any number of players to come in and out of the game at any time.

Even with that landmark change, it's not entirely clear whether the substitution rule was an impetus for change or merely a reflection of it. From 1946 to 1948, the rule in the NFL was that one could substitute three players at a time. While that prevented wholesale substitution, it did give the coaches some flexibility in bringing players in and out, getting them accustomed to the idea of rotating their personnel. In addition, the T formation, which had become the dominant offensive strategy in the league, made substitution more important than ever before. The game was played at a faster pace with the T–the 1952 NFL encyclopedia notes that the 1947, 1948, and 1949 seasons each saw new records set for the average number of plays per game.

"Reinforcements mean more in the games today than they ever did," opined a writer in discussing the Eagles' collection of linemen in a 1948 game program. "The fast-breaking T formation and the accent on passing–especially in the pro ranks–have speeded up the game considerably. There are more plays per game now than there ever were before, and it is the line which figures in every play, thus making the 60-minute lineman as rare as the good 5-cent cigar."

College football was also undergoing changes. Like the pros, the colleges had adopted the T formation en masse, increasing the impetus for platoon football. More important, the nation's colleges–like the NFL–had adopted unlimited substitution during World War II, but–unlike the NFL–retained it when the servicemen came home. In 1946, the nation's schools were being flooded with so many athletes that it made no sense to sharply restrict the number that could participate. The GI Bill, federal legislation meant to help returning soldiers get an education, was making it possible for more would-be athletes to go to college, and they were arriving on campuses in droves.

In his autobiography, Tom Landry described the scene at the University of Texas: "I arrived back in Austin for the 1946 spring semester to discover UT's enrollment had exploded. The same thing happened all over the country as millions of veterans on GI bills transformed the atmosphere on college campuses everywhere." With so much free talent available, college coaches found it easy to adopt two-platoon systems.

By 1949, many of the nation's colleges were turning out players who were used to playing only part of each game. Chuck Bednarik of the Eagles, Gordy Soltau of the 49ers, and Lou Creekmur of the Lions, all of whom turned pro in 1949 or 1950, all recalled being among the last to play 60-minute football at their colleges. (Ironically, the NCAA would adopt rule changes in 1953 making it conducive for players to play both ways. They backtracked in the following years, before finally restoring free substitution in 1965.)

Yet, it is important to understand that even if colleges had stopped turning out 60-minute men, they had not started turning out specialists. Many players had extensive experience at more than one position. For instance, a college player might be a starter at an offensive position and a backup at a defensive position. Or a player might play offense one season and defense the next. An offensive player might fill in for an injured defensive player, even playing both ways for a game or two. The colleges were still turning out players who were, for the most part, capable of playing more than one position. Professional coaches took advantage of this versatility.

Moreover, the notion of using 22 different players in one's starting lineup was an alien concept to most professional coaches of the era. Some didn't, at least at first, simply because it was a lot harder to find 22 (or 21 or 20 or . . .) good men than it was to find 11. Plus, it was standard procedure in those days for owners whose franchises were in bad shape financially to reduce their rosters to save money. By the end of the 1949 season, for instance, only 19 players were suiting up for Ted Collins' hapless New York Bulldogs. Playing both ways in a situation like that was inevitable.

More important, there was really no reason for coaches to restrict players to one position, one spot on the field, forever. The men coaching professional football in the Forties had grown up with a sport where everyone played offense and defense, where everyone was expected to be capable of playing on both sides of the ball. Many of the players in the NFL in 1949 had grown up with two-way football; their heroes were men like Bronko Nagurski and Marshall Goldberg and Bill Dudley and Sammy Baugh who did a multitude of things well. The ultimate compliment in those days was to say–as was said of Pete Pihos and Chuck Bednarik–that a player could have been a star at any position that he tried. When a player of that caliber walked on your field, you found him a spot.

Such was the case with the center-linebacker rotation of Bednarik, Lindskog, and Wojciechowicz. Greasy Neale in 1949 was blessed with the man he had called the best center in the league (Lindskog), as well as perhaps the two most famous college centers of the past generation. It would have made no sense to Neale to play just one of these outstanding talents: He rotated them to make use of all three.

This approach was reflected too in the way that Bears coach George Halas had legendary Notre Dame quarterback Johnny Lujack serve his apprenticeship to veteran superstar Sid Luckman by spending the 1948 season primarily at defensive back, where, by all accounts, he was quite a fine player. Or how Paul Brown, with no great need to use Cliff Lewis as Cleveland's quarterback, utilized him in the defensive backfield while having him spell Otto Graham occasionally. In 1948, Lewis threw eight passes but intercepted nine. In fact, Brown had no qualms about using his team's depth whenever he could. "Whenever timeouts permit wholesale substitutions," a *Sporting News* writer observed in 1947, "Brown uses a defensive group."

It's going a bit too far to say these stars were interchangeable parts, but it is correct to assert that they were thought of as players who could be used in a variety of ways without loss of effectiveness. In the world of unlimited substitution, however, there were others who lived rather nomadic existences. These were players who had athletic ability but no one outstanding skill. They might be switched from position to position to fill whatever leaks sprang up in the lineup. Such was the case of Jim Parmer, who played for the Eagles from 1948 to 1956.

"I could play halfback or fullback," Parmer recalled. "In fact, one year I started the first five ballgames that we played: I played one game at fullback, one game at halfback, one game at linebacker, one game at corner, and one game at safety. I could do about everything and none of it real well."

Parmer was far from alone in being shuffled about the field. Joe Sulatis, who played for the Giants and Yankees from 1943 to 1953, is listed as having played quarterback, fullback, blocking back, wingback, guard, defensive end, and linebacker. Still, these years did see the emergence of pro football's first real specialists. On offense, many of the earliest specialists were backs. One such player was Tony Canadeo of the Green Bay Packers.

In 1941, Canadeo joined the Packers from Gonzaga. On a team laden with such veteran superstars as Clarke Hinkle and Don Hutson, Canadeo soon became a two-way star. In 1943, playing tailback and defensive back, he threw the ball 129 times and ran with it 94 times, as well as returning 18 kicks, catching three passes, kicking three punts, and intercepting two passes in becoming an All-NFL player.

After World War II, his role started to become more specific. In 1947, the Packers installed the T formation on offense. "When they changed to the T, my God, it was like, you know, being on vacation. All I had to do was run with the ball," Canadeo recalled. Jack Jacobs took over the passing; the running was left to Canadeo and Walt Schlinkman.

By 1949, Canadeo, then 30, had also stopped playing defense. That season, his numbers went through the roof: He gained 1,052 yards rushing, becoming just the third person to gain more than 1,000 yards in a season.

"I think what helped more than anything to gain 1,000 yards was that we didn't have to play defense then. Going one way, it was easier to make 1,000 yards than when you had to go back and play defense," he recalled. That season, Canadeo carried the ball 208 times, but only handled it five other times (three receptions, two kick returns). Like Philadelphia's Steve Van Buren, he was showing what a player could accomplish if he concentrated solely on running with the football.

Even more notable was the effect that the platoon system had on defenses. For much of football's history, defenses had been a stepchild of offenses. A player was defined on the roster by his offensive position; players like Sammy Baugh, George McAfee and Otto Graham were all solid defensive players, but that was a bonus–their fame came about because of their abilities on offense. The All-Pro teams selected in the Forties consisted of 11 players selected at offensive positions; Bulldog Turner and Mel Hein were listed at center, not center-linebacker. In the era of two-play way, a player who was of little use on offense, was of little use *period.*

Once substitution arrived, things didn't change right away. It would take a few years for defensive specialists to attain any stature. In those years, it wasn't even easy to find out exactly who was playing defense. For instance, here is the listed starting lineup for the Philadelphia Eagles for the 1949 championship game:

RIGHT END: Pete Pihos. RIGHT TACKLE: Al Wistert. RIGHT GUARD: Bucko Kilroy. CENTER: Vic Lindskog. LEFT GUARD: Cliff Patton. LEFT TACKLE: Vic Sears. QUARTERBACK: Tommy Thompson. RIGHT HALFBACK: Bosh Pritchard. LEFT HALFBACK: Steve Van Buren. FULLBACK: Joe Muha.

Who played defense? Newspaper accounts and depth charts list only these 11 players as starters, and it's apparent that not all of them played defense. One has to look at the depth chart and try to figure out which substitutions were offensive-defensive switches.

One can make guesses, reasonably good ones. Jay MacDowell played defensive tackle; Chuck Bednarik and Alex Wojciechowicz played linebacker; and Frank Reagan, Dick Humbert, Pat McHugh, and Russ Craft played defensive back. But it's anybody's guess who spent how much time doing what, particularly on the line. Did Wistert play defensive tackle or did he yield to MacDowell? Did either of them yield to Mike Jarmoluk? Did Sears play the lion's share of the game at the other tackle spot, or did he yield to George Savitsky?

Who played middle guard? How did Muha fit in with Wojciechowicz and Bednarik at linebacker? What about Pihos, Ferrante, and Neill Armstrong at defensive end? This type of information is, for the most part, missing from accounts of Forties games. In baseball, scholars may be well on their way to accounting for every hit and every out in major-league history, but they'll never be able to account for every tackle in professional football history.

Still, players did start to get recognition for defensive play in the late Forties. There were two main types of defensive stars then: pass rushers and defensive backs.

One of the first notable pass rushers was Len Ford. A 6-foot-5, 260-pound end who was a walk-on at the University of Michigan, Ford joined the Los Angeles Dons in 1948 and spent two years with them, playing both offense and defense, before joining the Cleveland Browns. He had excelled on offense with the Dons, but Paul Brown had all the receivers he needed, so Ford became a defensive specialist.

In Cleveland, he quickly earned a reputation as something of an eccentric. "Lenny Ford, you know, he was a strange guy. Great big, strong, fast. He had a very high-pitched voice. . . . . Like a little girl talking," recalled Browns quarterback Otto Graham.

Detroit Hall of Famer Lou Creekmur remembered a game where Ford refused to take him on, leaving him with no one to block all day. Shortly thereafter, Creekmur saw Ford at the Pro Bowl and asked him why. Creekmur recalled Ford's answer: "He says, 'You dirty bastard, you broke my hand the week before and I wasn't coming in there and let you find out I had a broken hand.' "

Nevertheless, both Graham and Creekmur described Len Ford as a great defensive lineman. As a pass rusher, Ford's weapons were his strength and his ability to leap over blockers who got down low to try to stop him. A 1950 account by writer Mort Berry describes times in which Ford "simply hurled Detroit's offensive guard into the passer to bring both down."

Ford also had a knack for the ball, recovering 20 fumbles in his career. Those interviewed by Rick Korch for *The Truly Great* ranked him among the top 10 defensive ends in league history, as did coach George Allen in *Pro Football's 100 Greatest Players.* Calling him a "fast-moving mountain," Allen said, "Ford was the first great pass-rushing defensive end."

Ford's counterpart on the Eagles was John Green. A Tulsa graduate, he was cut by the Eagles on his first try, but made the team in 1947. Though he weighed just under 200 pounds, he soon became recognized as a disruptive force. In billing him as "probably the top defensive end" in the league in 1949, the Eagles described him this way: "Light but tough and wiry . . . seldom fooled . . . specialty blocking kicks." At that time, the Eagles paid a $10 bonus every time a player tackled the quarterback behind the line of scrimmage–it would be two decades before Rams defensive end Deacon Jones would coin the term "sack" to describe that occurrence–and nobody got more of those bonuses than Green.

"In watching the films of the games, it was just amazing to see this guy go in," recounted Al Wistert. "It looked like he had some sort-of a secret weapon in his hand because what he did to fullbacks . . . Johnny Green couldn't do that at 195 pounds . . . but he did it."

Green was also known as an eccentric, and Eagles official Jim Gallagher recalled that Green, who played from 1947 to 1951, basically dropped out of society after his career was over. He was never as famous as Len Ford, but Green's old teammates remembered him as a great defensive end.

"To block John Green all afternoon," recalled Jim Parmer, "was all the work that you wanted to do that day."

Ford and Green were a new type of weapon, and soon every team had to have one. By the mid-Fifties, the NFL was filled with hell-on-wheels defensive linemen—most of them closer in size to Len Ford than John Green—who breathed fire and swallowed quarterbacks for breakfast. Players like Gino Marchetti, Art Donovan, Doug Atkins, Ernie Stautner, Gene Brito, Andy Robustelli, Leo "The Lion" Nomellini, and Big Daddy Lipscomb. And by the mid-Fifties, teams had specialists in their secondary as well. The prototype for these was Emlen Tunnell of the New York Giants.

The 6-foot-1, 200-pound Tunnell had come to the Giants in 1948, asking for a tryout after serving three years in the Coast Guard and playing college football at Toledo (where he had suffered a broken neck) and Iowa. He became the team's first black player and immediately demonstrated a flair for hitting and for life in general—Paul Governali told writer Paul Zimmerman that he once saw Tunnell score a touchdown and proceed to twirl the ball on one finger and tap the ball back over his shoulder to an official. Tunnell saw limited duty on offense early in his career but then became a full-time safety. In 1967, he would become the first full-time defensive player elected to the NFL Hall of Fame, as well as the first black.

"Emlen changed the theory of defensive safeties," former Giants coach Jim Ray Howell told the New York Times at the time of Tunnell's death. "He would have been too big for the job earlier, and they'd have made him a lineman. But he had such strength, such speed and such quickness, I'm convinced he was the best safety ever to play."

"He was one of the guys that would just unload on you and level you," recalled Bears end Jim Keane. "He was quite a guy. He would level you."

Tunnell was a remarkable ballhawk. He piled up interceptions at record rates and held the NFL's career mark (79) for many years. He was also a top-notch kick returner, so good with the ball that his coaches were sometimes asked why they didn't play him on offense.

"He's more valuable to us right where he is," Giants coach Steve Owen once replied. "With Em on defense, we have the potential to have the ball on any play for the entire game."

Owen's statement indicated a changing approach to defense. Teams had started trying to place players in the secondary, rather than simply settling for those backs who weren't good enough to dislodge their best runners and passers from the lineup on offense. By 1949, Paul Brown had built a fine secondary around Cliff Lewis, Tommy James and Warren Lahr; they would combine for 108 interceptions in their professional careers. None of them are Hall of Famers, but all three can reasonably be said to be among the top defensive backs ever to play for the Browns.

At the same time, the Eagles had a quartet of backs who were pretty much full-time defenders. In an article about Pat McHugh in a 1949 Eagles game program, Dick Cresap of the Philadelphia Bulletin wrote: "McHugh, like Russ Craft, Dick Humbert and Frank Reagan, are the fellows you never see running the ball for the Eagles. They're strictly defenders, but fully as vital to the Birds' success as Tommy Thompson's passes or Pritchard's or Van Buren's running. They aren't big fellows, but they're fast as lightning and have the football savvy that anticipates where a play is heading."

The wording of this passage indicates an understanding that these players had distinct jobs that required distinct skills independent of any offensive ability that they might possess. But the article also reflected something of the ambivalence that players had about becoming specialists, even if it meant playing more than they would have otherwise. (Though both McHugh and Craft had scored touchdowns in the 1947 title game and made other contributions on offense over the years, neither was going to unseat Steve Van Buren.)

"Defense is all right," Cresap quoted McHugh as saying, "but I'm like any other player. Like to get my hands on that ball and run."

McHugh was not alone in his sentiment. Russ Craft, for instance, is a man who holds a share of an NFL record (interceptions in a game, four), who once returned a kickoff 103 yards, and who received numerous team and league honors in his nine-year NFL career. In his autobiography, Emlen Tunnell even named Craft to his all-time team as a defensive back. But atop the list of things that he's most proud of, Craft listed: "Being able to play both ways."

For players of this generation, playing both ways wasn't something to give up on easily. If they could find a way to get back in the game on the other side of the ball, they would.

"By 1948," recounted Eagles tackle Al Wistert, "I was playing primarily offensive tackle. Played some on defense but not too much. I can remember a game down in Washington against the Redskins, and Jay MacDowell, who was a fine defensive player, Jay, would go in on defense. So I said, 'Hey Jay, I haven't played any defense for a while. I'd like to get a shot at some defense. Next time we give the ball up and go over on defense, you just stay on the bench and let me in there. I'm gonna play a few plays.'

"I was playing the defense and then I made the tackle. And so then it was obvious to Coach that I was in there. And he turned around and said, 'MacDowell! What the hell is Wistert doing in there on defense?' He (MacDowell) says, 'He asked to play a little bit of defense.' . . . He (Neale) says, 'What the hell do you want him to do? You want him to get hurt or something? You go on in there!' "

"So," Wistert recalled, "MacDowell went back out on the field and said, 'Hey, Coach is raising hell. You better get out of here.' "

The culture of football being what it was at the time, one was supposed to frown on the idea of coming out of the game. As the years went on, players tried to hold on to their jobs on both sides of the line and mourned when they were converted to one-way players. Tackle Vic Sears, for instance, recalled when he was relegated to offense in 1951 after a decade of playing both ways. Sears, who claimed with great pride that he probably played more minutes in his career than any other Eagle ever did, felt deprived when he became a one-way player.

"Not playing defense," Sears recalled, "something was lost." The game, he said, simply wasn't as much fun.

"It did seem kind-of odd," recounted Bears end Ken Kavanaugh, whose career spanned both eras, "playing that way, only playing part of the game and sitting on the bench the rest of it. You do get out of the game."

Players did find ways to compensate for that sense of loss. For one thing, they got meaner. The years when two-platoon football came into vogue may have been the most vicious era in the history of the pro game. It was as if the standard for toughness had changed, from how long you could play to how hard you could hit.

There were any number of players in this era who were regarded either as heroes or hatchet men depending on which side of the line you were on. The Eagles, of course, had Bucko Kilroy and Chuck Bednarik, while Ed Sprinkle was a legend at end with the Bears. Pittsburgh had tackle Ernie Stautner, who was famous for clubbing people with a taped-up arm. "Ernie broke his arm in his rookie year and he wore the cast for the rest of his career," recounted Lions lineman Lou Creekmur.

Not all the hit men were linemen: Cardinals legend Charley Trippi once knocked Sprinkle out with a single punch, and there were few players more ornery or rugged than Rams quarterback Norm Van Brocklin. But the most infamous hitter of all was linebacker Hardy Brown, also known as "The Hatchet."

According to *The Pro Football Chronicle,* Brown had come out of a Texas orphanage and Tulsa University, joining the Brooklyn Dodgers in 1948 and then drifting from team to team before finding steady employment with the San Francisco 49ers at linebacker. He was a mere 6-foot-tall and weighed less than 200 pounds, but compensated for his size by pummeling his opponents.

"He was a middle linebacker, and he was really a tough guy," recounted Gordy Soltau, who played with Brown for several years. "Most running backs and receivers were always looking around to see where Hardy was before they started going. And he was an outstanding linebacker."

Brown's shoulder tackle was one of the deadliest moves that football has ever seen. He aimed his shoulder at the ballcarrier's face and broke noses, jaws, and cheekbones–anything that could be broken. How much damage he did is impossible to calculate, but stories such as Toy Ledbetter's account in *Iron Men* of how Brown severed the nerves in his cheekbone make it clear that Brown's legend has a factual basis. "He was one tough bastard," wrote former defensive tackle Art Donovan, no soft touch himself. "He had this knack, this technique of slamming a shoulder into a running back's face. . . . He was like a snake uncoiling."

Hardy Brown was a specialist. He broke faces.

******

In the week after Bednarik had his talk with Neale on the train, the Eagles had their first test of the 1949 season, a game against the Cardinals. The teams had gone in opposite directions since the 1948 championship game. The 100 new owners of the Eagles had hired Vince McNally as general manager and given Greasy Neale a contract extension. They then went on a buying spree, signing not only Bednarik, but also Arkansas running back Clyde "Smackover" Scott, an Olympic silver medalist in the high hurdles, and Notre Dame quarterback Frank Tripucka, who was billed as Tommy Thompson's heir apparent.

Tripucka didn't last long with the team (he was traded to Detroit early in the 1949 season) and Scott was slowed by injuries, but Bednarik toughened an already strong defense. The Eagles also acquired another University of Pennsylvania legend, Frank Reagan, from the Giants. Reagan, one of the league's leading interceptors, filled the void in the defensive secondary left by the retirement of Ernie Steele.

The Cardinals, meanwhile, had lost coach Jimmy Conzelman and back Marshall Goldberg to retirement and were having problems at quarterback because of Paul Christman's continuing injuries. With Buddy Parker and Buddy Handler coaching the squad, the teams played on Saturday Oct. 8, and the Eagles won, 28-3. Steve Van Buren gained 98 yards rushing and scored two touchdowns; Jim Parmer scored the other two.

For the Cardinals, it was a disastrous offensive performance. Christman and fellow quarterback Jim Hardy completed only seven of their 25 passes, while Charley Trippi was held to nine yards rushing on six attempts. The offense bounced back later in the season–they averaged almost 41 points per game during one incredible six-week stretch–but the Cardinals still finished in third place in the West at 6-5-1.

Having disposed of one of Chicago's NFL teams, the Eagles ran smack dab into the other one in the following game. The Bears, coming off a 21-16 loss to Los Angeles, blitzed the Eagles. Playing before more than 50,000 at Wrigley Field, the Bears won, 38-21.

The hero this time for the Bears was Johnny Lujack, who was filling in for Sid Luckman, sidelined with a thyroid condition. Lujack tossed two touchdown passes and scored a third. George McAfee contributed a 54-yard interception return, while rookie kicker George Blanda added a field goal. The formidable Bears line held Steve Van Buren to 18 yards rushing on 15 carries.

"It's funny, we always had good days against the Eagles," said Bears end Jim Keane, who had what he described as his best game as a professional that day, catching all eight passes thrown to him. The win improved Chicago's record to 3-1 and seemed to propel the Bears back into the hunt for the Western title. However, the Bears lost their next two games and found themselves struggling to catch the Rams.

The Eagles rebounded from the loss to Chicago with a pair of routs, beating the Redskins, 49-14, and the Steelers, 38-7. Both games saw franchise records set: Bosh Pritchard had a 77-yard touchdown run against the Redskins, while Clyde Scott had a 70-yard punt return against the Steelers. The win over Pittsburgh took the steam out of the surprising Steelers, who were now featuring rookie Joe Geri as the triple-threat tailback in the league's last single-wing offense. The Steelers won only two more games after their loss to the Eagles and finished a distant second to them in the East.

On Nov. 6, the Eagles had a heavily anticipated game against Los Angeles. The Rams were 6-0, with two victories over the Bears. Second-year coach Clark Shaughnessy had fashioned a formidable offense, utilizing a playbook that consisted of several hundred plays and a new formation. New acquisition Elroy Hirsch, formerly a halfback, was split wide, as was second-year end Tom Fears, while end Bob Shaw played tight to the line. This was the formation that was to become the standard NFL pro set: A quarterback, two running backs, two wideouts, and a tight end.

The 1949 Rams had highly regarded linemen Dick Huffman and Fred Naumetz, big-play backfield threats Verda "Vitamin T" Smith and

Jerry Williams, and workhorse fullback Dick Hoerner. They also had the first player ever drafted from a black college, rookie fullback-linebacker Paul "Tank" Younger of Grambling State. And they were blessed with two Hall-of-Fame quarterbacks: veteran Bob Waterfield and rookie Norm Van Brocklin.

In future years, the two would split the position fairly evenly, but in 1949, Waterfield did the lion's share of the passing. Still, the combative Van Brocklin gave the Rams another dimension on offense.

"Norm was a real fiery guy: Get in there and let's go for a bomb right away," recalled Elroy Hirsch. "Whereas Waterfield was the guy with strategy and 'Let's call four or five plays, and build up to something.'

"Norm had probably the stronger arm. Norm did our punting, so did Waterfield. Waterfield kicked extra points and field goals. They were both very valuable guys, but they were two different personalities. Waterfield would take a game plan and work it out to the T, whereas Norm would come in off the bench . . . and he'd go for broke. Bob was a little more conservative. Two great, great quarterbacks," Hirsch said.

Shaughnessy's offense could be exhilarating, but on Nov. 6 it went flat as the Eagles hammered the Rams, 38-14. "If yesterday's Eagles-Los Angeles game, for instance, was the 'playoff preview' it was cracked up to be, then the Rams needn't even show up for the post-season falderol," wrote the International News Service in its coverage of the game.

The game featured one of the more memorable defensive touchdowns in Eagles history: Defensive back Russ Craft stripped the ball from Hirsch after a reception and ran it 21 yards for six points. The Eagles offense didn't have its best game–Van Buren gained only 71 yards on 21 carries–but Neale's team knocked the only unbeaten team in pro football from its perch.

"There is something more permanent than change in pro football ranks–namely, the dynasties set up by the Cleveland Browns of the All American Conference and the Philadelphia Eagles of the National League," said the International News Service account of Philadelphia's win.

The loss sent the Rams into a tailspin. The following week, they needed a short touchdown run by Fred Gehrke with 24 seconds left to tie Pittsburgh. They tied the Cardinals in the following game to drop to 6-1-2. A 42-20 win over the Bulldogs improved their situation, but they then lost to the Cardinals, 31-27, to fall to 7-2-2. Entering the final week of the season, they were just percentage points ahead of the 8-3 Bears, who had won five straight with Johnny Lujack at the helm. That day, Lujack put extraordinary pressure on the Rams by throwing six touchdown passes and passing for a record 468 yards in a 52-21 rout over the Cardinals.

But the Rams got six touchdown passes of their own against Washington on the last day of the season, four from Van Brocklin and two from Waterfield. Bob Shaw caught four of the touchdown passes, while Tom Fears grabbed 10 passes to boost his season total to 77, topping the league record of 74 set by Don Hutson in 1942. The result was a 53-27 victory and the Western title.

The Eagles, meanwhile, rolled through their last five regular-season opponents to finish at 11-1. The star down the stretch was Steve Van Buren. In a 42-0 rout over the Bulldogs on Nov. 20, he carried the ball 35 times for 174 yards and two touchdowns. A week later, he set a team record that still stands, gaining 205 yards on 27 carries in a 34-17 victory over Pittsburgh.

He finished the season with 1,146 yards, breaking the league record he set in 1947. Playing offense exclusively for the first time, Van Buren carried the ball a league-record 263 times and ran for 11 touchdowns. In listing him, Pete Pihos, and Mac Speedie as the only unanimous selections on the 1949 Associated Press All-Pro team, the wire service quoted Greasy Neale as saying that Van Buren's only flaw was that "he runs over his own men when they get in his way."

On Dec. 18, there would be plenty of Rams for Van Buren to run over.

*****

"We're glad the Rams won the Western division title," Neale was quoted as saying in the program for the 1949 championship game. "We figure we can beat them easier than the Bears."

Cocky after their November victory over the Rams, the Eagles were looking forward to their third straight title game for another reason. The Rams played in a stadium that seated more than 90,000, and though there had not been much in the way of advance ticket sales, the teams anticipated a crowd of at least 60,000 people. Best of all, there was no chance that snow or ice would keep the crowds away. For the first time in recent years, the players' split of the championship game receipts seemed likely to be lucrative.

"We figured we'd go out there," recounted Philadelphia's Chuck Bednarik, "and if we could win, we'd each earn about three-four thousand dollars apiece, which was a big thing, believe it or not."

"We went out to California by train because Greasy Neale wouldn't fly. We stopped in Chicago, worked out; we stopped in Albuquerque, worked out; then we got to California. It was nice, the weather was nice."

But when the players woke up on the morning of the championship game, it was raining in Los Angeles. And raining and raining and raining. With only about 30 percent of the game's tickets sold and little prospect for any more, everybody's first instinct was to go back to bed and play the game another day.

"The field . . . had about 6 inches of water standing on it," recounted Eagles defensive back Dick Humbert. "There was mud all over, and it was a mud bowl, was what it turned out to be. Of course, the people didn't show up."

A postponement would require the approval of Bert Bell, who was back in Pennsylvania. The commissioner was contacted, but the word came back that the game had to be played because of radio broadcasting commitments. "The commissioner, who is 3,000 miles away," Rams owner Dan Reeves is supposed to have told his team, "informed us that radio commitments make a postponement impossible. According to Eagles guard Bucko Kilroy, the joke soon going around Los Angeles was, "What do the Liberty Bell and Bert Bell have in common? They're both cracked."

Not everybody painted Bell as the villain of the piece. According to Eagles tackle Al Wistert, Bell did lobby the NFL's other owners to postpone the game, but only if they would guarantee the championship gate in case fewer than 27,000 people bought tickets for the rescheduled event. The owners, of course, got no money from the championship game, so, according to Wistert, they refused.

Either way, the game did go on as scheduled, and the weather clearly hurt the Rams more than the Eagles. Shaughnessy's team found its passing game bogged down. Footing was bad, and the Eagles linebackers were using the conditions to help them do something they already did very well: Jam up the receivers at the line of scrimmage and keep them from getting up the field to catch the ball.

"All I know, it wasn't a day for an offensive end," recalled Elroy Hirsch. "Or a halfback. They were so tough defensively. Gosh they were tough. I remember the linebacker over me was Chuck Bednarik . . . I don't know if I got off the line of scrimmage. He held me. He was really effective."

The Rams never got started, but the Eagles were able to move the ball. In the second quarter, Tommy Thompson engineered a six-play, 65-yard drive. He completed three key passes on the drive: An 11-yard pass to Jack Ferrante, a 15-yard pass to Ferrante (caught on the ground after it had been deflected), and a 31-yard pass to Pete Pihos. Pihos' catch was the game's first touchdown, and Cliff Patton converted the extra point to give Philadelphia a 7-0 lead. Thompson completed only two other passes on the day, but had done enough to give the Eagles a lead.

The rain did not let up, and neither did the Eagles' defense. Four minutes into the third quarter, the Eagles' defense produced the game's second touchdown, scoring on a blocked punt. The hero was defensive end Leo Skladany, a rookie who had been signed from Paterson of the American Association to replace the injured John Green. The Rams were backed up to their 5, and Don Paul's center snap was high.

"No one bothered to block me because conditions were so awful," recounted Skladany. "Bob Waterfield was the punter, and luckily I managed to extend my body and get my hands on the ball just as it left his foot. I kept my balance, scooped up the ball on the 2-yard-line, dove into the end zone, and skidded almost 10 feet on my stomach."

Cliff Patton converted the extra point and the score was 14-0. With more than a quarter to play, the scoring was complete for the afternoon, though the Eagles did drive deep into Rams territory again, only to lose the scoring chance when Jim Parmer fumbled at the 7. The Eagles controlled the ball on the ground, with Van Buren carrying the ball 31 times for 196 yards, a championship-game record.

"Although he didn't figure in either of the scores, Van Buren, the Eagles' all-pro back, gave as great a running exhibition as the Coliseum has ever seen," said the Associated Press.

While Van Buren excelled, the Rams got nowhere. The team, as a whole, gained 21 yards on 24 rushing attempts, with Fred Gehrke leading the way with 13 yards on three carries. In the air, Bob Waterfield was 5 for 13 for 43 yards, while Norm Van Brocklin was 5 for 14 for 55 yards. The Rams never got closer than the 26.

"What was billed as a high-scoring duel between two speed-burning pass-happy teams turned into a slow-moving tug-o'-war between two lines, with the Eagles for the better," said the Associated Press.

For the Eagles, the win was their 22nd in their last 24 games. In that period, they had outscored their opponents, 719-241, posting eight shutouts. They had also become the only team to post back-to-back shutouts in championship games. No team has done it since.

Still, there were some disappointments. For a game in which players for both teams were hoping for a crowd of 60,000 or 70,000 or even more, a total of 22,245 people had shown up. That was 6,000 fewer than had sat through the snow game in 1948 and a few hundred less than had attended the AAFC's last game the week before. There would be no big payoff; the Eagles got only about $1,100 each for winning the title.

"We had been hoping and praying for years that this would happen, that the Rams would win in the West when we won in the East, when the game was to be played in the West. And it happened," recalled Al Wistert. "And then if it didn't start raining on Friday night . . . We thought, oh boy, we're gonna make a big paycheck, and we didn't."

It was a glorious and awful double shutout.

7

1950—PASSING POWER

****

Longtime Eagles official Jim Gallagher is fond of referring to it as the first Super Bowl. The matchup was a bold stroke by the newly reformulated NFL, pitting the two-time defending league champion against the only champion that the AAFC had ever had in the opening game of the season. The outcome, it's safe to say, was not what the old-line people in the NFL were expecting: Cleveland 35, Philadelphia 10.

The weather for this one was fine, and 71,237 people, paying as much as $4 each, bought tickets and packed Municipal Stadium in Philadelphia on Sept. 16 to see this clash of the titans. The Eagles had started out as 7-point favorites but the spread had evaporated in the weeks before the game because several Philadelphia stars were hurt. By game time, the Eagles were without tackle Al Wistert, halfback Bosh Pritchard, and, most important of all, halfback Steve Van Buren, who had broken a toe.

Still the Eagles and the city of Philadelphia were confident. After years of terrible teams, the city had grown use to dominance by the Eagles–their winning ways had even rubbed off on the Philadelphia Phillies, who were on their way to their first World Series in 35 years.

These were the lineups:

BROWNS starters: LE: Mac Speedie. LT: Lou Groza. LG: Abe Gibrson. C: Frank Gatski. RG: Lin Houston. RT: Lou Rymkus. RE: Dante Lavelli. QB: Otto Graham. LHB: Rex Bumgardner. RHB: Dub Jones. FB: Marion Motley.

Substitutions: LE: Jim Martin, George Young, Horace Gillom; LT: Darrell Palmer, John Kissell; LG: Weldon Humble, Alex Agase; C: Tommy Thompson, Hal Herring; RG: Bill Willis; RT: Forrest Grigg, John Sandusky; RE: Len Ford; QB: Ken Gorgal, Cliff Lewis; LHB: Warren Lahr, Ken Carpenter; RHB: Tommy James, Don Phelps; FB: Tony Adamle, Emerson Cole.

EAGLES starters: LE: Jack Ferrante. LT: Vic Sears. LG: Cliff Patton. C: Chuck Bednarik. RG: Duke Maronic. RT: Bucko Kilroy. RE: Pete Pihos. QB: Tommy Thompson. LHB: Clyde Scott. RHB: Frank Ziegler. FB: Jack Myers.

Substitutions: LE: John Green, Billy Hix; LT: Walt Barnes; LG: John Magee; C: Vic Lindskog, Alex Wojciechowicz; RG: Mario Giannelli, Barnes; RT: Jay MacDowell, Mike Jarmoluk, Walt Stickel; RE: Neill Armstrong, Norm Willey; QB: Bill Mackrides, Frank Reagan; LHB: Russ Craft; RHB: Jim Parmer, Pat McHugh, Joe Sutton; FB: Joe Muha, Willey.

The first significant play came very early in the first quarter. After going nowhere on their first three plays, the Eagles punted and Browns rookie Don Phelps returned the ball 69 yards for an apparent touchdown. However, a clipping penalty against Len Ford nullified the runback. Even worse for the Browns: Lou Groza, their peerless kicker, was injured on the play and had to leave the game.

A few minutes later, the Eagles put together the game's first good drive. They moved the ball 53 yards, mostly on runs by second-year backs Clyde Scott and Frank Ziegler. The Browns finally halted them at the 9 by batting away three Tommy Thompson passes. Cliff Patton then booted a 15-yard field goal to give the Eagles a 3-0 lead.

That lead didn't stand up for long. The Browns were not making any headway on the ground, but they were picking up yardage through the air. The Eagles' defenders were baffled by the precise routes that the Browns were running, and Blanton Collier's offensive linemen were holding their blocks long enough to give Otto Graham time to throw. Graham's first touchdown strike came late in the first quarter. It was to halfback Dub Jones, who was being covered by Russ Craft.

Graham recounted that Jones had "been going down running sideline patterns and so forth, and he came back one time and just simply said, 'He's ready.' And I knew just exactly what he meant." Jones had reasoned that Craft was now susceptible to a sideline fake.

"So he calls, fakes to the sideline, and takes off. I hit him for 60 yards and he makes a touchdown, and Russ Craft's going the wrong way," said Graham.

The pass to Dub Jones, actually 59 yards, gave the Browns a 7-3 first-quarter lead. Still, the Eagles held tough. They recovered a Marion Motley fumble and drove to the 2 before Motley showed the NFL what a dominating force he could be on defense. Motley stopped the Eagles at the line on three consecutive plays and forced them to surrender the ball without scoring. At this point, Cleveland began to dominate.

Later in the second quarter, Graham drove the Browns down the field again. Starting at the 29 after an interception by Cliff Lewis, Graham hit Mac Speedie for 10 yards and Motley for 20. Then after Motley went up the middle to the 26, Graham hit Dante Lavelli in the end zone. Lavelli's diving catch, followed by Forrest "Chubby" Grigg's second extra point, gave the Browns a 14-3 halftime lead.

The Browns took the second-half kickoff and scored again. Five straight completed passes brought the ball down to the Eagles 11. After an incompletion, Graham squirmed out of the grasp of rookie defensive end Norm "Wildman" Willey and hit Mac Speedie for a touchdown.

Clyde Scott had been Philadelphia's best weapon in the first half, rushing for 46 yards, but as the offense took the field in the third quarter, they were without the second-year back, who had separated his shoulder. Trailing 21-3 and now without his top *three* runners, Greasy Neale began tinkering with his offense. He employed Russ Craft as the principal runner in what the Philadelphia Inquirer described as a "z-wide formation, similar to a single wing." The Eagles drove to the Browns' 33 using that new formation, but the Browns intercepted a Tommy Thompson pass to halt the drive.

Later in the third quarter, new Eagles cornerback Joe Sutton, a Philadelphian who had played for the AAFC's Buffalo Bills, picked off an Otto Graham pass. Neale then put in Bill Mackrides in place of Thompson, and the hometown favorite got results. Mackrides hit Jack Ferrante and Jack Myers, then threw a 17-yard touchdown to Pete Pihos. It was 21-10, but it was also the last action Mackrides would see in the game.

"Things weren't going well with Tommy Thompson," Mackrides said in recounting Neale's maneuvering, "so he took him out and put me in just to see if he could change things and it did, but Tommy raised Cain with him, he wanted back in, so he put him back in. So I didn't get back in."

The Eagles didn't make any headway the rest of the day. The Browns, meanwhile, shifted gears and started running. At the beginning of the fourth quarter, they used Motley, Jones, and Rex Bumgardner to drive down the field before Graham scored on a 1-yard run. In the last minute of the game, Dub Jones broke free for 57 yards before being brought down by Frank Reagan. As the clock ran out, Bumgardner took a lateral from Graham and scored. Forrest Grigg, filling in for the injured Lou Groza, converted his fifth extra point to make the final score 35-10. The Browns were for real.

"We're happy," Paul Brown told reporters in a surprisingly quiet Browns dressing room after the game. "We're not going to gloat when we win a ballgame."

"They dominated us, there's no question about it," recalled Chuck Bednarik. "I was very much impressed by that Cleveland team. We read about 'em in the other conference, didn't really know how good they were, but I can tell you, I was impressed."

The loss left the city of Philadelphia stunned. "Joy may have returned to Mudville by this late date," began Frank O'Gara's account in The

Philadelphia Inquirer, "but there is none in Philadelphia today. The mighty Eagles have been knocked out."

*****

Cleveland's triumph had been built on preparation, both strategic and mental.

It's only a slight exaggeration to say that the Browns had been preparing for this game since 1946. They had long since run out of things to prove in the AAFC and had grown mighty tired of hearing how weak their league was. A few months before the contest, George Preston Marshall of the Redskins had said that the NFL's weakest teams could toy with the Browns. (Cleveland went on beat Washington the first nine times that they played.)

"I can tell you quite honestly that for four years, Paul Brown never even mentioned the NFL," recalled Otto Graham. "He just simply put those derogatory comments up on the bulletin board, and we read them every day or whenever them came out.

"I can honestly say in my opinion there was no team in the history of sports that was more prepared to play a game emotionally then we were that very first game in the NFL."

Added Lou Groza, "You know, we'd gonna through four years of all this stuff, of 'minor league.' Of course, we had a lot to prove, and we got started, we started a big score against the Eagles."

Beyond the emotional factor, Paul Brown had also scouted the Eagles extensively and thought long and hard about how to beat Greasy Neale's 5-2-4 defense. His solution was much like the one Cardinals Coach Jimmy Conzelman had come up with for the 1947 championship game: Attack the middle. Brown spread his offensive linemen wider than usual, send his ends wide, and then sent a back up the middle. Or he sent the backs into the flat–pulling the linebackers away–and then threw to an end in the middle of the field.

Brown also passed to his backs in the flat, forcing the Eagles linebackers to chase them from all sorts of awkward angles. And he utilized a variety of precision pass patterns, particularly along the sidelines.

Pretty soon, the Eagles defenders were so wary of the twists and turns that the receivers were taking that they got themselves faked out and were surrendering big gains. Greasy Neale's 5-2-4 had been exploited before, but no one had so thoroughly documented the ways to beat it as Paul Brown did that day.

*****

The Browns' victory that day opened the eyes of the NFL pretty quickly. The first coach to formulate a strategic response was Steve Owen of the Giants. Owen was in attendance when the Browns demolished his pal's defense, and he soon hatched an answer to Cleveland's offense. According to Tom Landry's autobiography, Owen went to his team's defenders and told them they were going to play a 6-1-4 defense when they faced the Browns on Oct. 1. The players were left to work the details out among themselves.

The Giants had substantially improved their team after finishing 6-6 in 1949. They had drafted fullback Eddie Price of Tulane, adding a new threat to an offense that had depended on quarterback Charlie Conerly and halfback Choo-Choo Roberts the previous year. And as part of the merger arrangement, they had added several players from the defunct AAFC Yankees. The most notable pickups were Arnie Weinmeister, a standout tackle from Canada; and three defensive backs, Harmon Rowe, Otto "The Claw" Schnellbacher, and Landry. That trio combined with Emlen Tunnell to give the Giants an enviable quartet in their secondary.

The 6-1-4 that Owen and his players devised made use of New York's four standout defensive backs without sacrificing strength in the middle. More important, the formation made unique use of the two defensive ends. On passing plays, the ends dropped back into coverage, giving the Giants a 4-3-4 formation. This guaranteed that at least one defender would be in whatever zone of the field Dante Lavelli and Mac Speedie headed into, making it hard for them to get open simply by faking out one man. And the tackles, Weinmeister and Al DeRogatis, were counted on to clog up the middle in case the Browns decided to depend on Marion Motley's power running.

The defense that the Giants utilized against Cleveland in that early-season game was not very sophisticated. But it was new and different enough to befuddle the Browns: Otto Graham threw three interceptions in completing only 12 of 30 passes, and Cleveland was unable to get past midfield until the second half. Sportswriters even *noticed* the new defense, observing that when the ends were back in coverage, the formation looked like an umbrella.

Using this so-called umbrella defense and a short touchdown run by Eddie Price, the Giants beat the Browns, 6-0. It was the first time Paul Brown's juggernaut had been held scoreless. More important, Steve Owen had reclaimed some of the pride that the NFL had lost when Cleveland put Greasy Neale's champions to shame.

For their rematch Oct. 22, Owen tried a variation on his new defense, a 5-1-5. This time, Otto "The Claw" Schnellbacher intercepted Otto Graham three times, and the Browns got their only points on two field goals by Lou Groza and a short run by Graham that followed a muffed kickoff return by Giants rookie Jim Ostendarp. The Giants, meanwhile, got second-half touchdown runs by Forrest Griffith and Joe Scott to win, 17-13, thus becoming the first team to defeat the Browns twice in a season.

"The Giants, who threw up an impregnable defense to stop Paul Brown's behemoths, 6-0, earlier in the month, outplayed the Browns again in every department and once again virtually silenced their biggest gun, peerless Otto Graham," said the International News Service account of the game.

But the Browns kept pace with the Giants by beating everyone else they played, and the Eagles joined the division race as well. Neale's team followed the crushing defeat to the Browns by humiliating the Cardinals, 45-7, eight days later. Their defense was devastating, intercepting quarterback Jim Hardy a league record eight times and forcing him to fumble twice. Russ Craft led the way with four interceptions and Joe Sutton had three.

The following week, the Eagles handed the Rams their worst defeat of the year, 56-20, at Municipal Stadium. Craft was the hero again, returning a kickoff 103 yards. On Oct. 29, with Joe Muha and John Green returning a pair of Sammy Baugh turnovers for touchdowns, the Eagles beat the Redskins and moved into first place in the American Conference with a 5-1 mark, one game ahead of both the Giants and Browns.

"After a shaky start," said the Associated Press account of the Eagles-Washington game, "the Eagles appeared today to be taking dead aim on their third straight National Football League title." It looked all the world like the team had righted itself, that the humiliating loss to the Browns was an aberration. That, however, did not prove to be the case.

*****

The Eagles went from first place to a 6-6 record. The downfall was swift and ugly.

Neale's team lost to the Steelers, 9-7, on Nov. 5 as Muha's 50-yard field goal attempt fell short on the last play of the game. They recovered to shut out the Redskins the following week, but lost their final four games, falling to the Cardinals once, the Browns once, and the Giants twice.

Each defeat was close and each was frustrating; for instance, the Browns scored their only touchdown in a 13-7 victory when Warren Lahr intercepted a pass intended for Steve Van Buren on a special pass play that Neale had designed. (Because the weather was bad, the Browns attempted only one pass that day, and that play was nullified by a penalty. After picking apart the Eagles in the opener, Otto Graham was officially 0-for-0 in the rematch.)

There were three basic causes for the Eagles' Sept. 16 loss to the Browns and their subsequent downfall. The first and most obvious was injuries, particularly the loss of Steve Van Buren. "My only excuse," said Chuck Bednarik of the opening-day loss to the Browns, was that "we didn't have Steve Van Buren. That's like them not having Otto Graham."

Van Buren did return to action soon after the opening game, as did Al Wistert. But Bosh Pritchard and Clyde Scott did not play again in

1950, and Van Buren was never quite himself again. He did lead the league in rushing attempts, but gained only 629 yards (sixth in the league) and averaged a mere 3.3 yards per carry. The broken toe had ruined his balance.

"I was done then, but I played a few more years. At the end, I was playing part of the time," recounted Van Buren. "Not at the end, but part of the time, I was playing with 12 shots of Novocain."

However, the injuries weren't in and of themselves fatal to the Eagles' chances. Another reason for the loss to the Browns was that Greasy Neale had refused to take Cleveland seriously.

"I know when we played them in the big game," recounted Bill Mackrides, "Greasy took them very lightly. I mean, we really didn't pay much attention to their defense and their offense. We did to some extent. But Paul Brown had been scouting us for a couple of years. He really knew what to do to stop us. And he did.

"I think Greasy was a great coach, no question about it. I think, what, if he had the feeling that this would be a team that would give us trouble, he would have worked harder, and we probably could have beaten them."

Neale, who was renowned for his willingness to listen to his players, even declined the advice of players who suggested that he should pay attention to the Browns.

"I went to see them play," recalled Al Wistert, "because I hurt my knee and while my knee was injured, I went to Cleveland and watched the Browns. Then when you'd come back and tell him some things that they were doing, he would say, 'Well they can't do that against us. They'll never do that against us. They can't do that' because he was very proud of his football team."

Neale's refusal to scout the Browns was particularly damaging when it came to pass defense. Unfamiliar with the precise patterns that Dante Lavelli, Dub Jones, and Mac Speedie were running, Neale's defensive backs found themselves turning the wrong way all day. He underestimated Cleveland's passing game and that cost him dearly.

Behind the scenes, there were other problems, some of them insidious. Dissension had reared its head on a team known for togetherness. Despite its signing spree before the 1949 season, the new ownership had not done much to win the respect of the players. Al Wistert spoke with contempt of the gift that the owners gave the players for winning the championship: Zippo cigarette lighters. "Now would you believe that? What would it cost? A dollar? 98 cents?" (Wistert recalled that the players decided that they should have something better to remember their title by and came up with the idea of having a championship ring. Joe Muha designed it, and it cost the players $65 each.)

After the merger of the two leagues, Philadelphia's owners told the players that they could not afford to give them raises for the 1950 season. The merger, of course, had ended the bidding war, but had not immediately solved the financial problems of teams that were not particularly profitable. Still, the players didn't want to hear it. They were still smarting from the disappointing take from the championship game in Los Angeles; some were no longer willing to stake their livelihood on good weather at the championship game.

"So we went to training camp that year," Alex Wojciechowicz told writer Myron Cope, "agreeing to play the season without a raise, but after we got there to that camp in Minnesota, we found there were six ballplayers who hadn't signed. There were six looking for raises. They were in camp, but they didn't suit up."

According to Wojciechowicz, Greasy Neale called Jim Clark and told him to either sign the six holdouts or send them home, because they were "standing around here leaving a bad taste in everybody's mouth." Clark then came to Minnesota and gave the holdouts raises. (Wojciechowicz may have exaggerated the number of holdouts, but both Pete Pihos and Frank Reagan were holding out when Clark showed up.) Everybody else got flat raises of $300, but the rest of the team assumed that the six holdouts had done far better than that. That, Wojciechowicz told Cope, was the team's downfall.

As the season progressed, relations between Neale and Clark deteriorated. Longtime Eagles official Jim Gallagher recalled the ownership was upset with what they perceived as Neale's reluctance to develop young talent. The trade of quarterback Frank Tripucka, a high-draft choice in 1949, particularly upset the owners.

The battle between Clark and Neale turned physical after one of the late-season losses to the Giants, apparently the 7-3 defeat at the Polo Grounds on Nov. 26. Accounts of the incident vary, but Clark apparently was critical of Neale's offensive strategy, and Neale was contemptuous of Clark's notion that he should have any say in the way that Neale ran his team. The two nearly came to blows. At the end of the season, Neale was fired. Despite ending his career with four consecutive losses, his career record was 66-44-5.

The players were not uniformly supportive of Neale–tackle Vic Sears said Neale's actions left Clark no choice–but it did mark the end of an era for the Eagles.

******

Using an assortment of defenses and scoring enough points to get by, Steve Owen's Giants team finished the 1950 season with a 10-2 mark. With Marion Motley leading the league in rushing, and Lou Groza setting a record for field goals in a season, the Browns also finished 10-2, setting up a Dec. 17 divisional playoff.

The third matchup of the Browns and Giants in 1950 was the most memorable. Once again, the Giants kept the Browns out of the end zone; this time, however, they couldn't get a touchdown of their own. With the Browns leading 3-0 in the fourth quarter, the Giants' Choo-Choo Roberts ran 32 yards to the Browns' 4 before being tackled from behind by Bill Willis. Charlie Conerly threw an apparent touchdown pass to Bob McChesney on third down, but a penalty nullified the score. After two more plays were wiped out by penalties, New York ballcarrier Joe Scott collided with a teammate and went down at the 13. The Giants had to settle for tying the game with a field goal.

The Browns then drove down the field, setting up a 28-yard field goal by Lou Groza with 58 seconds left. With time running out, Bill Willis thwarted the Giants' final chance by tackling Conerly in the end zone for a safety, giving the Browns an 8-3 win and the American

Conference title. In three games, the Giants had held Cleveland to one touchdown and intercepted Otto Graham seven times, but it was the Browns who made it to the championship game.

Their opponent was the Los Angeles Rams. After the loss in the 1949 championship game, Clark Shaughnessy had been fired and replaced by Joe Stydahar. The former Bears lineman scrapped Shaughnessy's Pro Set offense (it would be revived by the end of the decade), making Elroy Hirsch an end instead of a flanker and utilizing three running backs once again. Their new backfield weapons in 1950 included legendary Army star Glenn Davis, making his belated NFL debut at the age of 25, and huge "Deacon" Dan Towler, who would eventually be used with fellow heavyweights Tank Younger and Dick Hoerner in what came to be known as an "elephant backfield."

On offense the Rams were devastating. After beating Baltimore, 70-21, in an exhibition game, they defeated the hapless Colts, 70-27, on Oct. 22. In two games against each team, the Rams outscored the Packers, 96-28, and the Lions, 95-52. The team racked up an astonishing 466 points in 12 games–more points, for instance, than any NFL team scored in the 16-game schedule of 1995.

Statistically, they were off the charts. Norm Van Brocklin and Bob Waterfield were the league's top two passers, Tom Fears set NFL records by catching 18 passes in one game and 84 for the year, and Verda "Vitamin T" Smith ran three kickoffs back for touchdowns. The Rams, however, lost two games to the Bears and wound up tied with them in the National Conference at 9-3.

Halas' team was once again loaded with first-rate linemen, with AAFC refugee Dick Barwegan joining perennial stars Bulldog Turner, George Connor, Ray Bray, and Fred Davis. The team had some problems on offense, though, as Johnny Lujack experienced serious shoulder troubles. Lujack ran the ball well, but threw 21 interceptions and only four touchdowns. In the divisional playoff game between the Bears and Rams, Van Brocklin suffered broken ribs, but Waterfield, weakened by the flu, threw three touchdown passes to Fears to give Los Angeles a 24-14 victory. (From 1947 to 1950, the Bears won 36 of 48 regular-season games but did not reach a single championship game.)

11403-COHE

On Dec. 24, 1950, the Rams and Browns met in Cleveland for the championship. "The game started fast, ended wild, and looked like a pack of rabbits on amphetamine in between," said the NFL historians in *The First Fifty Years.* "Both teams scattered receivers all over the scrimmage line in an assortment of formations rivaled by few halftime bands."

On their first play, the Rams had Tom Fears break inside, drawing the attention of a linebacker. Glenn Davis broke free and caught a Bob Waterfield pass, which he toted 82 yards for a touchdown. Otto Graham brought the Browns right back, hitting Dub Jones for a 31-yard touchdown to cap a six-play drive. Los Angeles took the following kickoff and went 81 yards on eight plays. Dick Hoerner got the touchdown on a three-yard run. Before the fans had a chance to settle in their seats, the Rams had taken a 14-7 lead.

There was a brief respite before Cleveland's Dante Lavelli scored the last touchdown of the half. Lavelli, who would catch 11 passes on the day, hauled in a 37-yard touchdown from Graham in the second quarter. The Browns, however, failed to convert the extra point. Holder Tommy James was unable to catch the snap and ended up trying to throw the ball to Tony Adamle in the end zone. At the half, that errant snap was the difference in the game as the Rams led, 14-13.

Early in the second half, Graham hit Lavelli for a 39-yard touchdown, giving the Browns a six-point lead. The Rams responded with a display of power football. After completing three straight passes, Bob Waterfield gave the ball seven straight times to Dick Hoerner, who plunged over from the 1 on the last of those plays. On the first play after the ensuing kickoff, Marion Motley fumbled and Rams defensive end Larry Brink recovered. Brink ran 6 yards for another touchdown. The extra point by Waterfield gave the Rams an eight-point advantage.

Later in the third quarter, the Browns got a break. Defensive back Warren Lahr intercepted a Waterfield pass, and the Browns took over on their own 35. Graham completed five straight passes to Lavelli, then hit Rex Bumgardner for a 14-yard touchdown early in the fourth quarter. With almost a quarter to play, it was 28-27 in favor of the Rams.

Neither team made much headway for most of the final quarter.

With just over three minutes left, Graham fumbled and the ball was recovered by Rams linebacker Mike Lazetich. The Browns' defense, however, stiffened, and the Rams were forced to punt. Cliff Lewis returned the kick for Cleveland to the Browns' 32. With 108 seconds left in the 1950 season, Otto Graham went to work one last time.

Graham gained 14 yards on a run on first down, then completed passes to Bumgardner, Dub Jones, and Bumgardner again in quick succession. The last completion was Graham's 22nd of the day (Waterfield had 18 for the Rams) and put the ball at the 11. After a quarterback sneak picked up one more yard, the Browns brought in Groza, hero of the divisional playoff game, to try a 16-yard field goal. The kick was perfect. The Browns had won the NFL championship.

"We just ran out of gas, and they had a little left in their tank," recalled Rams end Elroy Hirsch.

Fans mobbed the Browns after the kick; Paul Brown's trademark felt hat was crushed during the victory celebration. Some fans even built a celebratory bonfire in the bleachers.

"Both teams were great," recalled Rams center Fred Naumetz, who was playing his last game that day. "Some of the greatest names in pro football took part on both teams."

The 1950 NFL title game was perhaps the greatest game in a season of great games.

*****

Three weeks after the title game, Graham locked horns with Waterfield and Van Brocklin again. This time, however, Philadelphia's Walter "Piggy" Barnes, Chuck Bednarik, John Green, Pete Pihos, and Al Wistert were on Graham's team as the NFL revived the Pro Bowl, an all-star game between the league's best players. And those five Eagles got to win: Waterfield threw three touchdown passes, but Graham outlasted him again, running for two touchdowns as the American (Eastern) Conference won, 28-27.

Wistert, who was the captain of the winning team, recalled that the game was beneficial in other ways–he got help on his blocking technique from Browns assistant coach Blanton Collier. " 'Wisty let me tell you something,' " Wistert recounted that Collier said to him. "And he gave me a little change of technique as far as my pass-blocking was concerned. With that I got into better position to block . . . than I ever had before."

Wistert's situation was an ironic one. Here was the most-honored tackle in the league, a tackle known for his peerless technique, getting advice–good advice–from an assistant coach on a team that Greasy Neale had not taken seriously only months before. In hindsight, one can take this as more evidence that the league was passing the Eagles by.

Still, the Eagles went about the business of trying to win football games. When the 1951 season began, Bo McMillin, Pete Pihos' old college coach at Indiana, was at the helm, but a number of familiar faces were missing. Alex Wojciechowicz, Jack Ferrante, Joe Muha, Cliff Patton, and Tommy Thompson had all either retired or been released. Stomach cancer forced McMillin to quit after two games, and former Redskins end Wayne Millner took over. With 23-year-old Adrian Burk at quarterback, the team sagged to 4-8.

Millner was fired after the season and replaced by Jim Trimble. Bobby Thomason was acquired from Green Bay to play quarterback, and the team drafted its first black players, running backs Ralph Goldston of Youngstown State and Don Stevens of Illinois. (Though they did not bring in black players until six years after the color line was broken, the Eagles were not the last NFL franchise to integrate. That dishonor went to the Redskins, who did not have a black player until 1962.)

The exodus of veterans continued under Trimble. Departing from the Eagles before the 1952 season were Al Wistert, Vic Lindskog, Mario Giannelli, Walter Barnes, Bosh Pritchard, Clyde Scott, Pat McHugh, Frank Reagan, and Neill Armstrong. On Aug. 3, in the team's first scrimmage, Steve Van Buren collided with a rookie guard and wrecked his knee. The playing career of the NFL's all-time leading rusher was over.

Trimble's tenure was not a disaster. In 1952, the Eagles finished 7-5, tied for second behind the Browns. Without Van Buren, the squad had no discernible running game, and their quarterbacks were nothing special, but Chuck Bednarik, Bucko Kilroy, Russ Craft, Mike Jarmoluk, Wildman Willey, and newcomer Wayne Robinson gave them a touch of the old quality on defense. They also had two exceptional young receivers, Bobby Walston and Bud Grant, a second-year player who had been good enough as a teen to play for Paul Brown on his Great Lakes military team in 1945.

In 1952, Grant finished second in the NFL in receptions to Cleveland's Mac Speedie. To utilize his young pass-catchers, Trimble moved Pete Pihos to defensive end, and Pihos made All-Pro on defense. After the season, Grant joined a growing exodus of NFL players to the Canadian Football League, and Pihos returned to offense.

Trimble never really improved on his first year with the Eagles. In 1953 and 1954, the Eagles finished second to the Browns with records of 7-4-1 before falling in 1955 to 4-7-1. The team lacked the overall quality of the Browns but did have some outstanding individual performers. Pihos actually had the best years of his career from 1953 to 1955, leading the league in receptions in each of those years. In 1955, Pihos concluded the season by catching 10 passes against the Cardinals and 11 passes against the Bears, and then retired.

Along with Pihos, linemen Mike Jarmoluk, John Magee, and Bucko Kilroy also retired after the 1955 season. Back Jim Parmer departed after the 1956 season, leaving Chuck Bednarik as the last player from the championship teams still playing for the Eagles.

Of all the players on the two Eagles title teams, Frank Tripucka kept playing longer than any of them, playing in Canada until 1959 and then quarterbacking the Denver Broncos in the new American Football League for their first four seasons. (They later retired his jersey number.) Bucko Kilroy, meanwhile, remained in the NFL into the 1990s, spending more than a half-century as a player, coach, consultant, scout, and executive. In 1992, the commissioner paid tribute to him in his 50th year in the NFL, noting that most of the league's franchises had joined the NFL after Kilroy did.

History was kind to the members of the championship-era Eagles. In 1965, Van Buren's stature was confirmed by his inclusion in the first group of NFL Hall of Fame inductees from the post-World War II era.

He was soon joined by Chuck Bednarik (1967), Alex Wojciechowicz (1968), Greasy Neale (1969), and Pete Pihos (1970).

"I went in with Otto Graham and Sid Luckman and Bob Waterfield," Van Buren recalled. "They must have thought I was a quarterback."

******

As the Eagles struggled, the Browns continued to make history. No player accomplished more than Otto Graham.

The 1950 season had demonstrated that a sophisticated passing game could win. This notion was anathema to the game's purists—West Point coach Red Blaik was quoted that year as saying, "I do not concede that an uninterrupted succession of passes is football." Still, it was hard to argue with the results. The Fifties were dominated by the league's top quarterbacks.

In 1951, Graham picked up where he had left off as the Browns coasted to 11 straight wins following a season-opening loss to the 49ers. Brown's juggernaut held four opponents scoreless and made effective use of an assortment of offensive weapons. In a game against the Bears on Nov. 25, one of Graham's favorite targets, Dub Jones, became only the second player to score six touchdowns in an NFL game. Their two toughest games again were against the Giants; they won 10-0 and 14-13. Defensive tackle John Kissell preserved the second win for the Browns with two late goal-line stops.

The Browns got new respect around the NFL in 1951. Dub Jones, Lou Groza, Frank Gatski, Len Ford, Tony Adamle, and Warren Lahr all were named to All-Pro teams for the first time Alas, another of the team's stars, Marion Motley, wrecked his knee that year in a collision with Adamle during practice. His skills diminished, Motley hung on with the Browns through 1953.

That same season, Rams quarterback Norm Van Brocklin set a single-game passing record that still stands, passing for 554 yards against the Yankees, while Elroy Hirsch had his greatest year, catching 17 touchdown passes and leading the league in reception yardage over San Francisco's Gordy Soltau by an astounding 669 yards. Waterfield and Van Brocklin were again league leaders in passing, while three of the team's running backs (Dan Towler, Tank Younger, Dick Hoerner) averaged more than 6 yards per carry.

The championship game was a rematch between the Rams and Browns. Like the 1950 game, it was exciting and dramatic, with an array of offensive weapons on display. The Browns took a 10-7 halftime lead but that didn't last. As he did in the 1950 title game, Rams defensive end Larry Brink made a key play in the third quarter, forcing Otto Graham to fumble. Andy Robustelli recovered for Los Angeles, setting up a touchdown run by Dan Towler. Bob Waterfield tacked on a field goal a few minutes later, giving the Rams a 17-10 lead.

Graham then led the Browns on another legendary drive, taking them 70 yards for a score, a 5-yard touchdown by Ken Carpenter, that tied the score at 17 deep in the fourth quarter. Less than a minute later, however, Norm Van Brocklin hit Tom Fears at midfield as Cleveland defensive backs Tommy James and Cliff Lewis collided. Fears ran the rest of the way for a 73-yard touchdown and the winning score.

The title would be the only one the Rams would win in Los Angeles. They were dethroned in 1952 by the Detroit Lions, a team that was awakening from a slumber that had lasted more than a decade. The Lions moved back into the title chase when they acquired a first-rate quarterback–raucous, intense, hard-drinking Bobby Layne.

The Lions had added Layne and two Heisman Trophy winners, SMU running back Doak Walker and Notre Dame end Leon Hart, in 1950, but it wasn't until Buddy Parker took the reins in 1951 that the team became a force to be reckoned with. Parker's other offensive weapons included end Cloyce Box and former Cardinals back Pat Harder. Jack Christiansen led a first-rate secondary, and the Lions were loaded with fine linemen, including Lou Creekmur, Dick Stanfel, Thurman "Fum" McGraw, ex-Cardinal Vince Banonis, and the enormous Les Bingaman.

This was a never-say-die team; teammate Doak Walker often said that Layne never lost a game, he just ran out of time occasionally. In 1952 and 1953, Layne led the Lions to championship game victories over the Browns.

"Otto (Graham) was probably one of the premier quarterbacks," recalled Creekmur, a six-time All-Pro. "He was a better quarterback in basics and everything else than Layne. He could throw the ball better; he could throw a better pass. He was probably more intelligent than Layne, he could fake better than Layne, many, many things.

"But nobody," Creekmur continued, "had the guts of a Bobby Layne. And the determination, the competitive spirit that Bobby Layne had. . . . Fans used to hate us because they'd leave, and we'd come ahead and win the ballgame."

Layne's numbers were not eye-catching. In the 1952 divisional playoff game with the Rams and title game with the Browns, he threw a total of four interceptions but no touchdowns. Still, the Lions won both games to claim the NFL title. Detroit capitalized on Cleveland's injury woes–Mac Speedie, Dub Jones, and John Kissell missed the title game–as well as mistakes in the kicking game by punter Horace Gillom, returner Ken Carpenter, and kicker Lou Groza, who was playing with cracked ribs. Final score: Detroit 17, Cleveland 7.

Bob Waterfield retired after the 1952 season, but Graham, Layne, and Van Brocklin were at the top of their games in 1953. Despite the loss of Speedie to the Canadian Football League, Graham led the league in passing and guided the Browns to wins in their first 11 games before a season-ending 42-27 loss to the Eagles.

Van Brocklin, Hirsch, Towler, end Bob Boyd, and back Skeet Quinlan were all among the NFL's leaders in various offensive categories, but the 1953 Rams still finished behind Layne and the 10-2 Lions. In a rematch of the 1952 title game, Layne led the Lions on an 80-yard drive late in the game for a 17-16 victory over the Browns. Layne hit Jim Doran for a 33-yard touchdown to cap the drive. Doak Walker converted the extra point for the winning margin, and Carl Karilivacz intercepted Graham's final pass to seal the win.

Paul Brown's aging Browns were sluggish as 1954 began. They lost two of their first three games, yielding 55 points to an apparently harmless Pittsburgh team in Week 3. But Graham proved to have not one but two last hurrahs in him. The team won eight in a row to win their conference, then destroyed the Lions by a score of 56-10 in their third consecutive title game matchup.

Graham retired, but he came out of retirement just before the 1955 season started to lead the Browns back to the title game against the Rams. The Browns won that game, 38-14, and Graham retired for good. Paul Brown ended a chapter in his autobiography with a description of Graham's final NFL moments: "I brought Otto out of the game and that huge crowd of Rams fans stood and gave him a thunderous ovation–a rare tribute to an opposing player, but certainly appropriate to this man's greatness . . . Though we tried, we never found another Otto Graham."

In his final two NFL title games, "Automatic Otto" threw for a total of five touchdowns, including a 50-yarder to Dante Lavelli, and ran for five more. In 10 seasons, he had led the Browns to 10 championship games, winning seven. His supporting cast had changed a great deal–Frank Gatski, Lou Groza and Lavelli were the only other Browns to stick around for the full decade–but Graham was just as effective working with Ray Renfro, Kenny Konz, Mike McCormack and the team's other new stars as he had been with the 1946 cast.

He would land in the Hall of Fame in 1965, to be followed in succeeding years by Paul Brown (1967), Marion Motley (1968), Groza (1974), Lavelli (1975), Len Ford (1976), Bill Willis (1977), McCormack (1984) and Gatski (1985). If a quarterback is to be judged primarily on how successful his teams are, then Graham has to be rated as one of the best of all time, if not the best.

*****

With Graham, Layne and Van Brocklin leading the way, football suddenly seemed to be a world of spectacular aerial gunners, any one of whom could turn around a game on one play. "I came in when football game was just really uptempo," recalled Richard "Night Train" Lane, a cornerback who joined the Cardinals in 1952. "A lot of good throwers."

Lane set an NFL record by intercepting 14 passes in his rookie season and quickly joined New York's Emlen Tunnell and Detroit's Jack Christiansen as one of the league's top defensive backs. Lane, whose nickname came from a jazz song and who later married singer Dinah Washington, became one of the first purely defensive players to be treated like a star. By the middle of the decade, defensive units also started to have followings. Nicknames came into vogue–the front wall of the Eagles during the mid Fifties was billed as the "Suicide Seven."

Layne's Lions boosted the first famous defensive secondary: Built around Christiansen and Yale Lary, this group became known as "Chris' Crew." In New York, the Giants faithful paid tribute to the entire unit by chanting "Dee-fense, dee-fense" as they took the field. (As obvious as this may seem now, apparently nobody had thought to do this before the mid-1950s.)

The new attention paid to defensive players was part of a natural response on the part of coaches to the dynamic passing games. These aerial attacks had scared the holy heck out of teams, making it evident that a new philosophy of defense was needed. The guiding light in this respect was Steve Owen of the Giants. He had taken the defense of his pal Greasy Neale and revised it so that it had the best of both worlds: strength up the middle and flexibility in the secondary.

"It is virtually indisputable," argued writer Tom Bennett, "that Owen's umbrella emerged from Neale's Eagle defense, that they huddled together to discuss mutual tactics against Cleveland in 1950, and that the 4-3 defense of later years evolved from the strategy of both men."

Yet, as Bennett and others have suggested, Owen's new formations weren't as significant as the new approach to defense that they suggested. The old style of defensive play–one in which each defender basically responded to the actions of the man he was responsible for–made it easy for the offense to isolate a defender and exploit him. With the old style of play, the offense always set the tone, and the defense simply had to hope it was good enough to stop whatever the offense threw at it.

Owen's defense was one in which defenders were expected to attempt to figure out what was going on and get there before it happened.

This new approach called for the defensive players to dictate their own movements; they could go where they thought they ought to go. This made playing defense more difficult–a player had to learn how to interpret what the offense was doing–and a player could be badly burned if he guessed wrong.

But this new sophistication was also rewarding. If the defenders could collectively interpret the movements and tendencies of the offensive players, they had a better chance of stopping intricate passing games. In time, this rethinking of defensive strategy led to the adoption of the 4-3-4 as the standard defense in the NFL. With its highly mobile linebackers, the 4-3-4 was an ideal formation for teams trying to "read" offenses and successfully pursue the play. In 1957, the 49ers added another wrinkle: the blitz. They sent their linebackers full steam after Giants quarterback Charlie Conerly to disrupt the play as it was starting. A few years later, coaches started sending defensive backs after the quarterback as well.

The middle linebacker was the field general of the 4-3-4, charged with reading the play, pursuing ballcarriers from sideline to sideline (or stuffing them at the line of scrimmage if they came up the middle), and hammering them ferociously. He took the shortest possible route to the ball, and–to steal a line from hockey coaching legend Fred Shero–arrived in ill humor. Middle linebackers Bill George of the Bears, Joe Schmidt of the Lions, Sam Huff of the Giants, and Bill Pellington of the Colts became stars in the Fifties. By the mid-Sixties, middle linebackers such as Ray Nitschke and Dick Butkus were as famous as any offensive player.

"A game which had once resembled a gang fight in a closet now had 22 fast men colliding in all corners of the field," said the NFL historians writing in *The First Fifty Years* about the evolution of defensive play. "Ballcarriers used to have one man at a time to worry about. Now they drew crowds of tacklers the way fresh meat draw piranhas. Defense was striking back."

As the game became more sophisticated and exhilarating, professional football grew ever more prosperous. Average attendance increased in 1950 and continued to rise every year of the Fifties. After a series of poorly attended championship games, attendance rose to 57,522 for the Rams-Browns rematch in 1951 and topped 48,000 for the rest of the decade.

Television continued its courtship of the sport, and the NFL's presence on television increased dramatically throughout the decade. In 1951, the Du Mont network televised the championship game nationally for the first time; in 1954, NBC took over from the failing network and paid the league a fee of $100,000 to do so.

Two years later, CBS started telecasting regular season games nationally. It would be years before Americans saw the likes of the Bud Bowl and the All-Madden team, but the sport now had exposure comparable to what major league baseball was getting.

"It was really just there. You never made a big to-do about TV," recalled Lou Creekmur.

Still the Lions All-Pro admitted that television coverage did create a new type of excitement about the sport.

"It was just fine that finally a lot of my friends and family could get to see me back East on Thanksgiving day. That used to be the big event, when I was playing, all my friends back in Jersey and Virginia could finally get to see you play."

With the destructive battle with the AAFC at an end, the league had time to consolidate its gains. After the Dallas Texans moved to Baltimore in 1953, the league was stable for seven seasons, with the same 12 teams playing in the same cities through the 1959 season. This was in a decade when such storied baseball franchises as the Brooklyn Dodgers, the New York Giants, and the Philadelphia Athletics were relocating in an effort to save themselves.

The players still had some leverage. The Canadian Football League started spending large sums of money for American players and attracted such notables as Mac Speedie, John Kissell, Tex Coulter, Gene Brito, Eddie LeBaron, John Henry Johnson, and Arnie Weinmeister. (Nine seasons after leaving the Eagles for the AAFC's 49ers, Bruno Banducci left the 49ers for Canada.) The spending habits of the Canadian league at least partially offset the demise of the AAFC and kept salaries at earlier levels. And with the rise in championship-game attendance, those big playoff shares that the members of the 1949 Eagles dreamed about finally became a reality.

It would be an exaggeration to say that professional football had fully arrived by the mid-1950s. There was still room for some great leaps forward and they would come in time. Running back Jim Brown arrived in Cleveland in 1957. and became perhaps the game's most visible star. Another milestone was the 1958 championship game, in which a Baltimore Colts quarterback named Johnny Unitas used television to show the nation what a great game this was. There would be others in the 1960s and 1970s: the rise of a new American Football League, the birth of the Super Bowl, Bart Starr's touchdown dive for Vince Lombardi's powerhouse Packers in the so-called "Ice Bowl," the boasts of a cocky quarterback named Joe Namath and his performance in Super Bowl III, the "Immaculate Reception" by Steelers rookie Franco Harris. All of these things would help football, according to the Gallup Poll, supplant baseball as America's favorite sport by 1972.

But the men who played and coached in the years 1946 to 1950 had set the wheels in motion. In that time, professional football had entered into virtually uncharted territory–West Coast football, integration, television, new strategies on offense and defense, scientific approaches to coaching, and, most important of all, two-platoon football–and grown. Though the men that played and coached during those years did not welcome all of these changes, and though the progress the sport made in those years was in fits and starts, there was no denying that professional football was finally on sturdy legs and ready for a greater destiny.

POSTSCRIPT: RUGGED AND ENDURING

****

Chuck Bednarik had a last hurrah with the Eagles in 1960. "Concrete Charlie" had spent much of the Fifties playing both ways for a series of weak Eagles teams, earning a reputation for his dedication and for his hitting.

"If not actually dirty, Bednarik was mean," wrote George Allen in picking him as the greatest linebacker of all time, as well as one of the best centers. "He did what he had to do and if he hurt people along the way, I guess he just accepted it. When he tackled them, they stayed tackled . . . He drew a bead on opponents and battered into them with frightening force."

In 1960, with former 49ers coach Buck Shaw at the helm and former Rams star Norm Van Brocklin at quarterback, the Eagles had their best team in a decade. By that year, Bednarik was exclusively a center. But in a game Oct. 23 against the Browns, an injury to Bob Pellegrini forced him into the lineup at linebacker at well.

"Lo and behold, Pellegrini goes down and Buck Shaw, out of the clear blue sky, tells me to get in. So I went in. Chuck Weber was our middle linebacker. He called the plays, defensive plays, and he told me . . . what I had to do in case it was a pass play," Bednarik recalled. "I played just about the entire game with him telling me what I had to do in the event of a pass play."

Bednarik went back to playing one way as the Eagles jumped out in front in the Eastern Division with a 6-1 mark, but got another chance to play both ways in a crucial game on Nov. 20 against the Giants. The Giants, who were right behind the Eagles with a 5-1-1 mark, built a 10-0 lead. Bednarik had started the game at outside linebacker, but after Giants middle linebacker Sam Huff gave Eagles center Bill Lapham a hard time in the first half, Bednarik started the second half at center. "The picnic's over," Bednarik told Huff on the first play. "The men are here."

When the Eagles took a 17-10 lead, Buck Shaw put Bednarik back into the game at linebacker. Late in the game, the Giants were driving when Bednarik crunched Giants ballcarrier Frank Gifford, separating him not only from his senses but also from the football. Chuck Weber recovered the fumble, and Bednarik stood over the unconscious Gifford, celebrating the game-winning play. A photograph of the moment earned Bednarik the everlasting wrath of Giants fans, but also sealed his mystique.

The Eagles finished 10-2 and wound up in the championship game against Vince Lombardi's resurgent Green Bay Packers. Lombardi's running offense was considered stodgy and old-fashioned, but a superb offensive line and fine set of backs made it work. In the title game, the Eagles overcame some early turnovers to beat the Packers, 17-13, in what would be the only loss ever inflicted on a Lombardi team in a championship game.

Bednarik played more than 58 minutes that day. "I didn't run down on three kickoffs, but I played every play offensively, every play defensively, and snapped" on kicks, he recounted. In the waning seconds of the game, Bednarik tackled Green Bay back Jim Taylor as he headed toward the end zone for what would have been the winning score. He sat on Taylor until the clock ran out.

Eleven years after the mud bath in Los Angeles, Bednarik and the Philadelphia Eagles had another NFL championship. Football had changed extensively since Bednarik's rookie year, but the glory still belonged to those who played it the best.

THE GAME I PLAYED

Some final thoughts on what it was like to play pro football in the Forties and early Fifties in the words of men who did. All quotes come directly from correspondence or interviews with me.

NEILL ARMSTRONG: The Eagles were a close-knit family in those days, including our wives and kids.

CHUCK BEDNARIK: Take, for example, Lawrence Taylor. What the hell can Lawrence Taylor do? OK, Lawrence Taylor's a good linebacker. Period. Lawrence Taylor can't do nothing else besides that. Lawrence Taylor never played both ways . . . He doesn't know what it feels like to stay in a game the entire game and really suck . . . Even (Dick) Butkus, as great as he was, that's all he did.

JIM BENTON: Today . . . you got guys playing football that, you know, if they had to play defense, they'd be dead ducks. You know, they just wouldn't be able to play.

GEORGE BLANDA: Great era.

CHARLIE CONERLY: I don't know if I'd enjoy playing like they do now. You know, every play, they have a different player go in. . . . I wouldn't want to run in and out, play one play every series.

RUSS CRAFT: One thing I will always believe: They don't play any harder than we did back in the old days.

LOU CREEKMUR: Today, you've got so many specialists that all a guy can do is block on pass protection, all a guy can do is block for the run, or all a guy can do is play defense and play the pass. Things such as this. We just stayed in there. (laughs) Big difference.

BILL DUDLEY: Immediately after the war and the emerging of the All American Conference, pro football took on a new meaning. The teams started traveling first class and training camps were likewise. The age of specialization began to appear and in 1946, I was one of the few football players that played *extensively* both ways.

JACK FERRANTE: Back in our days, you had to be good because there wasn't that many teams around . . . (Today), as long as you got two legs and two arms, they're gonna let you play because you know they need the manpower. Some of those guys aren't that good.

FRANK GATSKI: Every day was like Christmas.

MARIO GIANNELLI: I played for the Eagles in 1948-49-50-51. . . . Those four years were happy and enjoyable–made a lot of friends there. Living conditions were very good.

MARHSALL GOLDBERG: Football in those years was a means to end. You were establishing yourself in the society where you were living in the hopes of gaining an opportunity to make a livelihood. You couldn't live on the money that you're making in football. Many of us, myself included, were able to make connections. . . . All during the years when I was playing football I was working. I would go to work in the morning and then go to football practice in the afternoon.

OTTO GRAHAM: It's too bad that every individual in the world . . . couldn't play football. You learn very quickly it makes no difference whether the guy next to you is black, white, Protestant, Catholic, Jewish, whatever, Muslim, atheist, whatever. As long as he does the job and he's a decent person, that's all that counts, you know. . . . We wouldn't have these wars if everybody could play football.

JACK HINKLE: If every kid today, that's playing pro football today, could get along with their teammates as we did at that time, I know there's lot of stuff, you know, today with the blacks and the whites and all this crap. . . . It was just one great bunch of guys.

DICK HUMBERT: We played because we liked the game. It wasn't all the money we were making, you know. That was another thing I think was pretty important. We didn't have a stockbroker book under our arm. . . . We didn't make that much. But we liked the game. I guess we played because we just wanted to see how well we could play and how good we might be and how good the team might be.

WELDON G. HUMBLE: One of the most vivid things I remember about the Browns of 1946-1950 was the college-like attitude that we all had. It was an 'entire-team effort.' We all respected each other, as well as the team rules set by Paul Brown.

KEN KAVANAUGH: It's a whole different ballgame now. Gosh, these receivers can run down and they can't even touch 'em anymore. Gosh, I used to go out for a pass back when I was playing . . . you couldn't get off the line of scrimmage. They'd tackle you and grab you, throw you on the ground, and the officials never called holding or anything.

FRANK "BUCKO" KILROY: We traveled together in trains and buses and planes. I think there was great togetherness with the team . . . Maybe because we won. Maybe that was the reason. I don't know what it was. It really helped.

MAL KUTNER: Professional football in my day, though paying far less in gratuities than is the case today, nevertheless, provided the athlete with a (cash) nest egg to get a start in the business world. This was particularly true of my generation as the war had just ended, and with many people coming out of the services at the same time, jobs were at a premium.

DANTE LAVELLI: The important thing in the Forties was the camaraderie of the players–they took pride in being the best in their positions. My opponents and teammates became lifelong friends. The war years made the men different.

GEORGE McAFEE: David, I feel that I came into the game at a good time and I would not trade my years with the Bears for all the money the players are making now.

JIM PARMER: When I came up as a rookie, I was about to wet my pants. I was scared every day that I would do something wrong that would get me sent home. And I had to make that ballclub. We just flat did not have any money. . . . My wife and baby went home to live with their mother, and every day I would write my wife, and say, "Well, they brought in three more running backs, I guess I'll be coming home." And she would fire a letter right back at me the next day, "Don't you come home, we don't have any money. You make that ballclub." I would have killed somebody to have made that ballclub. And I think I really mean that.

CLIFF PATTON: We lived with each other just like brothers.

LOU SABAN: The most memorable moments, outside of playing, were the old facilities which in themselves carried a carload of memories. Ebbets Field, Polo Grounds, Kezar Stadium. . . . Great names and people. Now gone. What a waste of history.

CLYDE SCOTT: I'm saddened to think I wasn't able to participate at full force. . . . I wish I'd been healthy the whole time. Looking back and remembering the guys I played with, those were great years. It was the beginning of television, for one. For the first time, we saw ourselves on television.

ALLIE SHERMAN: There's a lot of great ballplayers who played in those times who just on the basis of physical size wouldn't be invited to a pro training camp, even though they have their skills.

GORDY SOLTAU: It's a life in itself to be a pro football player. And once you have been a pro football player, you'll always be. And you have certain camaraderie with those who shared your experience that no one else ever would have. So that part is a very precious thing in our lives. . . . You're so close for so long a period of time and you experience the same thing, the heights and the falls and the frustrations and the exhilaration. I guess the emotional part of it is as big as the physical.

ED SPRINKLE: The era you indicate for your research is right after the war. Pro football exploded–teams were added, crowds went up. Teams used airlines for transportation for the first time.

ERNIE STEELE: It was a good life. We enjoyed it.

WOODY STRODE: To think that I lived to see a linebacker get 1 million dollars a year and he don't have to touch the ball.

"DEACON" DAN TOWLER: The most memorable recollections I have about my career as a professional football player were the experiences I shared with my teammates.

WALLY TRIPLETT: Pro football before the TV era was a team game, and hatred between teams was normal, as was hatred of opposing team players.

AL WISTERT: Most all the guys, as soon as the football season was over, went to other jobs. And as a matter of fact, maybe even during the football season worked at other jobs to make ends meet, because, you didn't make that much money playing football.

EPILOGUE

In 1945, the NFL was composed of the Boston Yankees (coached by Herb Kopf), Chicago Bears (George Halas, Luke Johnsos, Hunk Anderson), Chicago Cardinals (Phil Handler), Cleveland Rams (Adam Walsh), Detroit Lions (Gus Dorais), Green Bay Packers (Curly Lambeau), New York Giants (Steve Owen), Philadelphia Eagles (Greasy Neale), Pittsburgh Steelers (Jim Leonard) and the Washington Redskins (Dud DeGroot).

These are some of the changes and some of the highlights of the next five years:

1946

New teams: NFL: Cleveland Rams became Los Angeles Rams. AAFC: Brooklyn Dodgers (coached by Mel Stevens, then Cliff Battles), Buffalo Bisons (Red Dawson), Chicago Rockets (they had five coaches during the season), Cleveland Browns (Paul Brown), Los Angeles Dons (Dud DeGroot), Miami Seahawks (Jack Meagher, then Hamp Pool), New York Yankees (Ray Flaherty), San Francisco 49ers (Buck Shaw)

New coaches: NFL: Jimmy Conzelman (Cardinals), Turk Edwards (Washington), Jock Sutherland (Pittsburgh). George Halas once again became sole coach of the Bears.

New (NFL): The NFL ended an experiment with free substitution, limiting substitution to three players at a time. Rosters were increased from 33 men to 35, then cut back to 34. Punts kicked into the end zone could now be returned.

Impressive NFL stat: Jim Benton (Rams) caught 63 passes, almost twice as many as anyone else.

Impressive AAFC stat: Chuck Fenenbock (Dons) led the league in yards per carry and yards per punt return.

Best records: NFL: Bears (8-2-1), AAFC: Browns (12-2)

Worst: NFL: Lions (1-10), AAFC: Seahawks (3-11)

Champions: Bears, Browns

1947

New teams: The AAFC's Miami Seahawks became the Baltimore Colts, and the Buffalo Bisons changed their nickname to the Bills.

New coaches: NFL: Clipper Smith (Boston), Bob Snyder (Los Angeles). AAFC: Cecil Isbell (Baltimore), Jim Crowley, then Hamp Pool (Chicago), Mel Hein & Ted Shipkey (L.A.)

New (NFL): Sudden death overtime was added for championship games. A back judge was added. A bonus pick was added to the NFL draft. One team each year would select a special choice at the beginning of the first round, relinquishing a late-round choice. This lasted until 1958.

Impressive NFL stat: Sammy Baugh (Redskins) piled up 2,938 yards passing and 25 TD passes.

Impressive AAFC stat: Spec Sanders (Yankees) ran for 1,432 yards and 18 touchdowns.

Best records: NFL: Cardinals (9-3), Browns (12-1-1)

Worst: NFL: Giants (2-8-2), AAFC: Rockets (1-13)

Champions: Cardinals, Browns

1948

New coaches: NFL: Bo McMillin (Detroit), John Michelosen (Pittsburgh), Clark Shaughnessy (L.A.). AAFC: Ed McKeever (Chicago), Jim Phelan (L.A.), Red Strader (N.Y.), Carl Voyles (Brooklyn)

New (NFL): Rosters were increased to 35 men. A flexible artificial tee was allowed for kickoffs. Plastic helmets were banned. Officials were given white penalty flags and whistles instead of horns. They were also required to meet before the game for a conference on rules, and their dressing room was made off-limits to coaches and owners before a game.

Also, Rams back Fred Gehrke, who had been a technical illustrator during the war, painted emblems on his team's helmets, a new concept that was soon to catch on.

Impressive NFL stat: Dan Sandifer (Redskins) intercepted 13 passes.

Impressive AAFC stat: Glenn Dobbs (Dons) averaged 49.1 yards per punt.

Best records: NFL: Cardinals (11-1), AAFC: Browns (14-0)

Worst: NFL: Lions (2-10), AAFC: Rockets (1-13)

Champions: Eagles, Browns

1949

New teams: The NFL's Boston Yankees became the New York Bulldogs. The AAFC's New York Yankees absorbed the Brooklyn Dodgers. The AAFC's Chicago Rockets changed their name to the Hornets.

New coaches: NFL: Charley Ewart (New York), Phil Handler & Buddy Parker (Cardinals), John Whelchel, then Herman Ball (Washington). AAFC: Clem Crowe (Buffalo), Walt Driskill (Baltimore), Ray Flaherty (Chicago)

New (NFL): Unlimited substitution was adopted on trial basis. Plastic helmets were permitted. Rosters were reduced again, to 32 men.

Impressive NFL stat: Steve Van Buren (Eagles) ran for 1,146 yards.

Impressive AAFC stat: Mac Speedie (Browns) had 1,028 yards on 62 receptions.

Best records: NFL: Eagles (11-1), AAFC: Browns (9-1-2)

Worst: NFL: Bulldogs (1-10-1), AAFC: Colts (1-11)

Champions: Eagles, Browns

1950

New teams: When the leagues merged, the Buffalo Bills, the New York Yankees, the Chicago Hornets, and the Los Angeles Dons ceased to be. The NFL's New York Bulldogs became the new New York Yankees. Two years later, the franchise moved to Dallas, then to Baltimore where it replaced a Colts team that died in 1951.

New coaches: Curly Lambeau (Cardinals), Buddy Parker (Detroit), Gene Ronzani (Green Bay), Joe Stydahar (L.A.). Also, Red Strader, who had coached the AAFC's Yankees, took over the NFL's Yankees, which had been the Bulldogs in 1949.

New: Unlimited substitution (see 1949) was made permanent. The teams were divided into the National and American conferences. The Pro Bowl was revived. In earlier years, the champion had played a team of all-stars. Now, two teams of all-stars played.

Impressive stat: Tom Fears (L.A.) caught 84 passes.

Impressive post-AAFC stat: Marion Motley (Browns) averaged 5.8 yards per carry.

Best records: Giants (10-2), Browns (10-2)

Worst: Colts (1-11)

Champion: Browns

*****

THE BEST PLAYERS

Enshrined in Canton: At the conclusion of the 1945 season, there were 17 active players who would be elected to the NFL Hall of Fame. Mel Hein, Arnie Herber, Don Hutson, and Wayne Millner all retired at the end of the year. Sammy Baugh, Tony Canadeo, Bill Dudley, Bruiser Kinard, Sid Luckman, George McAfee, Ace Parker, Ken Strong, Joe Stydahar, Clyde "Bulldog" Turner, Steve Van Buren, Bob Waterfield, and Alex Wojciechowicz remained active for at least one more year.

These are the Hall of Famers who joined them in professional football in following seasons:

1946 (7): Frank Gatski, Otto Graham, Lou Groza, Elroy "Crazy Legs" Hirsch, Dante Lavelli, Marion Motley, and Bill Willis.

1947 (2): Pete Pihos and Charley Trippi.

1948 (8): George Connor, Tom Fears, Len Ford, Bobby Layne, Joe Perry, Y.A. Tittle, Emlen Tunnell, and Arnie Weinmeister.

1949 (5): Chuck Bednarik, George Blanda, Jim Finks, Tom Landry, and Norm Van Brocklin. Finks was elected as an executive, and Landry as a coach.

1950 (5): Lou Creekmur, Art Donovan, Leo Nomellini, Ernie Stautner, and Doak Walker.

Additional players from this era may still be elected. Mac Speedie, Al Wistert, Marshall Goldberg and Charlie Conerly are the most likely.

Here are some additional measures of the era's top players:

ALL-PRO SQUADS

1946 (AP selections from both AAFC and NFL):

ENDS: Jim Benton (Rams), Jim Poole (Giants).

TACKLES: Al Wistert (Eagles), Bruiser Kinard (AAFC Yankees).

GUARDS: Riley Matheson (Rams), Bill Radovich (AAFC Dons).

CENTER: Clyde "Bulldog" Turner (Bears).

BACKS: Bob Waterfield (Rams), Glenn Dobbs (AAFC Dodgers), Spec Sanders (AAFC Yankees) Ted Fritsch (Packers)

The seven NFL players listed above were selected to the All-NFL squad. Other members of the NFL squad: tackle Jim White (Giants), guard Len Younce (Giants), and backs Sid Luckman (Bears) & Bill Dudley (Steelers).

Radovich was beaten out on the All-AAFC team by Bill Willis of the Browns and Bruno Banducci of the 49ers. Other members of the AAFC squad were ends Alyn Beals (49ers) and Dante Lavelli (Browns), tackle Martin Ruby (Dodgers), center Robert Nelson

(Dons), and backs Otto Graham (Browns) & Marion Motley (Browns)

1947 (AP selections from both AAFC and NFL):

ENDS: Mac Speedie (AAFC Browns), Bruce Alford (AAFC Yankees).
TACKLES: Al Wistert (Eagles), Dick Huffman (Rams).
GUARDS: Riley Matheson (Rams), Bruno Banducci (AAFC 49ers).
CENTER: Bulldog Turner (Bears).
BACKS: Sid Luckman (Bears), Steve Van Buren (Eagles), Otto Graham (AAFC Browns), Spec Sanders (AAFC Yankees)

The six NFL players listed above were also selected to the All-NFL squad. The NFL team also included ends Ken Kavanaugh (Bears) and Mal Kutner (Cardinals), guard Buster Ramsey (Cardinals), quarterback Sammy Baugh (Redskins) and tailback John "Johnny Zero" Clement (Steelers).

Except for Alford, the AAFC players listed above were also selected to the AAFC squad. Others on that team were end Dante Lavelli (Browns), tackles Lou Rymkus (Browns) and Nathan Johnson (Yankees), guard Bill Willis (Browns), center Robert Nelson (Dons), and backs Marion Motley (Browns) & Chet Mutryn (Bills)

1948 (AP selections from both AAFC and NFL):

ENDS: Mal Kutner (Cardinals), Mac Speedie (AAFC Browns).
TACKLES: Dick Huffman (Rams), Bob Reinhard (AAFC Dons).
GUARDS: Buster Ramsey (Cardinals), Dick Barwegan (AAFC Colts).
CENTER: Bulldog Turner (Bears).
BACKS: Steve Van Buren (Eagles), Otto Graham (AAFC Browns), Marion Motley (AAFC Browns), Charley Trippi (Cardinals).

The six NFL players listed above were also selected to the All-NFL squad. The NFL team also included end Pete Pihos (Eagles), tackle Fred Davis (Bears), guard Chuck Drulis (Bears), and quarterbacks Tommy Thompson (Eagles) & Sammy Baugh (Redskins).

Joining the five listed AAFC players on the AAFC squad were end Alyn Beals (Browns), tackle Lou Rymkus (Browns), guard Bill Willis

(Browns), center Robert Nelson (Dons), and backs Chet Mutryn (Bills) and John Stryzkalski (49ers).

1949 (AP selections from both AAFC and NFL):

ENDS: Pete Pihos (Eagles), Mac Speedie (AAFC Browns).

TACKLES: Dick Huffman (Rams), Arnie Weinmeister (AAFC Yankees).

GUARDS: Buster Ramsey (Cardinals), Dick Barwegan (AAFC Colts).

CENTER: Fred Naumetz (Rams).

BACKS: Steve Van Buren (Eagles), Otto Graham (AAFC Browns), Bob Waterfield (Rams), Chet Mutryn (AAFC Bills)

The six NFL players listed above were also selected to the all-NFL squad. The NFL team also included end Tom Fears (Rams), tackle George Connor (Bears), guard Ray Bray (Bears), and backs Tony Canadeo (Packers) & Elmer Angsman (Cardinals).

Joining the five listed AAFC squad were end Alyn Beals (49ers), tackle Bob Reinhard (Dons), guard Visco Grgich (49ers), center Lou Saban (Browns), and backs Frankie Albert (49ers) and Joe Perry (49ers)

1950 (AP, UPI or both):

ENDS: Tom Fears (Rams), Mac Speedie (Browns), Dan Edwards (Yankees).

TACKLES: George Connor (Bears), Arnie Weinmeister (Giants).

GUARDS: Bill Willis (Browns), Dick Barwegan (Bears), Joe Signiago (Yankees).

CENTER: Chuck Bednarik (Eagles), Clayton Tonnemaker (Packers).

BACKS: Johnny Lujack (Bears), Doak Walker (Lions), Marion Motley (Browns), Joe Geri (Steelers)

ALL-PRO SQUAD OF THE FORTIES

This team was chosen in 1969 by the Hall of Fame Selection Committee. Of note is the inclusion of Al Blozis, a tackle for the Giants who was killed in World War II.

END: Jim Benton, Jack Ferrante, Ken Kavanaugh, Dante Lavelli, Pete Pihos, Mac Speedie, Ed Sprinkle.

TACKLE: Al Blozis, George Connor. Frank "Bucko" Kilroy, Buford

"Baby" Ray, Vic Sears, Al Wistert.

GUARD: Bruno Banducci, Bill Edwards, Buster Ramsey, Bill Willis, Len Younce.

CENTER: Charley Brock, Bulldog Turner, Alex Wojciechowicz.

QUARTERBACK: Sammy Baugh, Sid Luckman, Bob Waterfield.

HALFBACK: Tony Canadeo, Bill Dudley, George McAfee, Charley Trippi, Steve Van Buren, Byron "Whizzer" White.

FULLBACK: Pat Harder, Marion Motley, Bill Osmanski

A number of Forties stars are on the team for the Fifties:

Tom Fears, Elroy Hirsch, Dick Barwegan, Chuck Bednarik, Otto Graham, Norm Van Brocklin, Bobby Layne, Joe Perry, Lou Groza, Len Ford and Emlen Tunnell. No one was picked for both teams.

ENCYCLOPEDIA TEAM

The 1952 version of the league's encyclopedia contained an all-time "consenus of opinion" team selected by Roger Treat. It's included here because it shows how the stars of the Forties, many of whom were still active, were regarded. I was surprised to see Vic Lindskog listed.

END: Don Hutson & Bill Hewitt. 2. Lavern Dilweg & Ray Flaherty. 3. Wayne Millner & Guy Chamberlain. Honorable mention: George Halas.

TACKLE: Wilbur Henry & Cal Hubbard. 2. Fred Davis & Russell Behman. 3. Glen Edwards & Joe Stydahar. HM: Roy Lyman & Steve Owen.

GUARD: Mike Michalske & Danny Fortmann. 2. George Musso & Walt Kiesling. 3. Bill Willis & Ray Bray. HM: Riley Matheson & Hunk Anderson.

CENTER: Mel Hein. 2. Bulldog Turner. 3. Nathan Barrager. HM: George Trafton & Vic Lindskog.

QB: Sammy Baugh. 2. Bob Waterfield. 3. Sid Luckman.

BACKS: Paddy Driscoll, Bronko Nagurski & Dutch Clark. 2. Ken Strong, Bill Dudley & Ernie Nevers. 3. Red Grange, George McAfee & Clark Hinkle. HM: Cliff Battles, Johnny Blood, Ernest Caddel, Tony

Canadeo, Tuffy Leemans, Verne Lewellen, Jim Thorpe, Steve Van Buren.

50TH-ANNIVERSARY TEAM

This team was chosen in 1969 by the Hall of Fame Selection Committee:

QB: John Unitas. FB: Jim Brown. HB: Gale Sayers. FLANKER: Elroy Hirsch. SPLIT END: Don Hutson. TE: John Mackey. TACKLE: Cal Hubbard. GUARD: Jerry Kramer (who has yet to be selected for the Hall of Fame itself). CENTER: Chuck Bednarik. KICKER: Lou Groza. DE: Gino Marchetti. DT: Leo Nomellini. LB: Ray Nitschke. CB: Night Train Lane. SAFETY: Emlen Tunnell. "THE LEGEND": Jim Thorpe

75th-ANNIVERSARY TEAM

Another officially sanctioned all-time team, greatly augmented and revised from the last one. (This time, apparently, they couldn't figure out what to do with Jim Thorpe.)

QUARTERBACK: John Unitas, Joe Montana, Sammy Baugh, Otto Graham.

RUNNING BACK: Bronko Nagurski, Marion Motley, Steve Van Buren, Jim Brown, O.J. Simpson, Walter Payton.

WIDE RECEIVER: Don Hutson, Jerry Rice, Lance Alworth, Raymond Berry.

TIGHT END: Mike Ditka, Kellen Winslow.

TACKLE: Roosevelt Brown, Anthony Munoz, Forrest Gregg.

GUARD: Jim Parker, John Hannah, Gene Upshaw.

CENTER: Mel Hein, Mike Webster.

DEFENSIVE END: Gino Marchetti, Deacon Jones, Reggie White.

DEFENSIVE TACKLE: Bob Lilly, Joe Greene, Merlin Olsen.

LINEBACKERS: Dick Butkus, Ray Nitschke, Willie Lanier, Lawrence Taylor, Ted Hendricks, Jack Ham, Jack Lambert.

DEFENSIVE BACKS: Night Train Lane, Ronnie Lott, Larry Wilson, Ken Houston, Mel Blount, Mike Haynes, Rod Woodson.

SPECIALISTS: Jan Stenerud, Ray Guy, Gale Sayers, Billy "White Shoes" Johnson

THE SPORTING NEWS TEAM

On Sept. 14, 1987, the Sporting News published two all-time teams selected by their readers. The voting was divided into two eras, with 1950 as the dividing line. This was the pre-1950 team:

END: Don Hutson, Dante Lavelli.

Ken Kavanaugh was 4th, Mac Speedie 5th, Pete Pihos 6th, Ed Sprinkle 8th, Jack Ferrante 12th, Mal Kutner 14th.

TACKLE: George Connor, Cal Hubbard

Frank "Bucko" Kilroy was 3rd, Vic Sears 8th, Al Wistert 10th

GUARD: George Musso, Grover "Ox" Emerson

Bill Willis was 3rd, Bruno Banducci 4th, Buster Ramsey 7th.

CENTER: Bulldog Turner.

Alex Wojciechowicz was 3rd.

QUARTERBACK: Sammy Baugh

No one else was within 2,500 votes, though Sid Luckman was 2nd, Bob Waterfield 3rd.

HALFBAÇKS: Red Grange, Jim Thorpe

Steve Van Buren and Charley Trippi were a distant 3rd and 4th. George McAfee was 7th and Bill Dudley 9th.

FULLBACKS: Bronko Nagurski

Marion Motley was 2nd, Pat Harder 5th.

Some Forties stars were on the ballot for the modern team:

END: Elroy "Crazy Legs" Hirsch (8th) and Tom Fears (21st)

TACKLE: Lou Groza (7th)

CENTER: Chuck Bednarik (2nd) and Frank Gatski (6th)

QUARTERBACK: Otto Graham (5th), Bobby Layne (9th), Y.A. Tittle (11th) and Norm Van Brocklin (14th)

RUNNING BACKS: Joe Perry (25th)

DEFENSIVE ENDS: Len Ford (13th)

SAFETY: Emlen Tunnell (4th)
KICKERS: Lou Groza (3rd)

GEORGE ALLEN'S STARTING LINEUP

There are several references in the text to an all-time top 100 selected in a 1982 book by George Allen, legendary coach. Here is his starting lineup. (Allen converted players to "modern" positions when it suited him.)

WIDE RECEIVER: Don Hutson, Lenny Moore
TIGHT END: Pete Pihos
TACKLE: Jim Parker, Forrest Gregg
GUARD: Danny Fortmann, Ron Mix
CENTER: Mel Hein
QUARTERBACK: Sammy Baugh
RUNNING BACK: Jim Brown, O.J. Simpson, Bronko Nagurski
DEFENSIVE END: Deacon Jones, Gino Marchetti
DEFENSIVE TACKLE: Bob Lilly, Leo Nomellini
MIDDLE GUARD: Bill Willis
LINEBACKER: Chuck Bednarik, Bill George, Dick Butkus
CORNERBACK: Herb Adderley, Night Train Lane
SAFETY: Jack Christiansen, Emlen Tunnell
KICKER: George Blanda
PUNTER: Sammy Baugh

BIBLIOGRAPHY

PLAYERS WHO PROVIDED INFORMATION

Years are seasons that they played in NFL or AAFC. Type of contact is indicated. Interviews were conducted by telephone. All quotes within the text come from these letters or interviews, unless otherwise noted. NFL hall of famers are marked with an asterisk

Frankie Albert, 1946-1952, 49ers, letter

Neill Armstrong, 1947-1951, Eagles, two letters

*Chuck Bednarik, 1949-1962, Eagles, interview 4/28/93

Jim Benton, 1938-1947, Rams-Bears, letter, interview 10/28/95

Angelo Bertelli, 1946-1948, Dons-Rockets, interview 2/5/94. (Bertelli died 6/26/99.)

*George Blanda, 1949-1958, 1960-1975, Bears-Oilers-Raiders, letter

*Tony Canadeo, 1941-1944, 1946-1952, Packers, interview 6/6/93

Charlie Conerly, 1948-1961, Giants, interview 12/28/93. (Conerly died 2/12/96.)

Leon Cook, 1942, Eagles, letter with clippings

Russ Craft, 1946-1954, Eagles-Steelers, two letters

*Lou Creekmur, 1950-1959, Lions, two letters, interview 6/5/93

*Bill Dudley, 1942, 1946-1951, 1953, Steelers-Lions-Redskins, letter

Jack Ferrante, 1941, 1944-1950, Eagles, letter, interviews 3/28/93 & 11/29/93

*Frank Gatski, 1946-1957, Browns-Lions, letter, interview 6/5/93
Mario Giannelli, 1948-1951, Eagles, letter
Marshall Goldberg, 1939-1943, 1946-1948, Cardinals, letter, interview 7/21/93
*Otto Graham, 1946-1955, Browns, letter, interview 5/27/93
Visco Grgich, 1946-1952, 49ers, sent letter & clippings
*Lou Groza, 1946-1959, 1961-1967, Browns, interview 6/24/93. (Groza died 11/29/2000.)
Jack Hinkle, 1940-1941, 1943-1947, Giants-Eagles, letter, interview 5/30/93
*Elroy "Crazy Legs" Hirsch, 1946-1957, Rockets-Rams, letter, interview 6/30/93
Lindell L. Houston, 1946-1953, Browns, phone call, sent letter & clippings. (Houston died 9/8/95.)
Dick Humbert, 1941, 1945-1949, Eagles, letter, interview 6/17/93
Weldon G. Humble, 1947-1950, 1952, Browns-Texans, letter
Mike Jarmoluk, 1946-1955, Bears-Yankees-Eagles, letter
Ken Kavanaugh, 1940-41, 1945-50, Bears, interview 5/11/94
Jim Keane, 1946-1952, Bears, interview 4/20/94
Frank "Bucko" Kilroy, 1943-1955, Eagles, interview 5/28/93
Mal Kutner, 1946-1950, Cardinals, letter
*Richard "Night Train" Lane, 1952-1965, Rams-Cardinals-Lions, letter
*Dante Lavelli, 1946-1956, Browns, letter
Vic Lindskog, 1944-1951, Eagles, interview 6/24/93
Bill Mackrides, 1947-1951, 1953, Eagles, interview 6/3/93
Baptiste Manzini, 1944-1945, 1948, Eagles, two letters
*George McAfee, 1940-1941, 1945-1950, Bears, letter
Max Morris, 1946-1948, Rockets-Dodgers, phone call
Fred Naumetz, 1946-1950, Rams, letter
Jim Parmer, 1948-1956, Eagles, letter, sent two cassettes of recollections
Cliff Patton, 1946-1951, Eagles-Cardinals, phone calls, letter
*Pete Pihos, 1947-1955, Eagles, letter
Lou Saban, 1946-1949, Browns, letter
John Sandusky, 1950-1956, Browns-Packers, letter, interview 7/19/93

Clyde Scott, 1949-1952, Eagles-Lions, letter, interview 5/26/93
Vic Sears, 1941-1953, Eagles, interview 3/31/93
Allie Sherman, 1943-1947, Eagles, interview 9/27/93
Leo Skladany, 1949-1950, Eagles-Giants, letter
Gordy Soltau, 1950-1958, 49ers, letter, interview 8/15/93
Ed Sprinkle, 1944-1955, Bears, letter
Ernie Steele, 1942-1948, Eagles, interview 5/11/93
Woody Strode, 1946, Rams, interview 3/10/94. (Strode died 12/31/94.)
Johnny "Strike" Strzykalski, 1946-1952, 49ers, letter
"Deacon" Dan Towler, 1950-1955, Rams, letter
Wally Triplett, 1949-1950, 1952-1953, Lions-Cardinals, two letters
Frank Tripucka, 1949-1952, 1960-1963, Eagles-Lions-Cardinals-Texans-Broncos, letter, interview 7/9/93
*Steve Van Buren, 1944-1951, Eagles, interview 7/19/93
Al Wistert, 1943-1951, Eagles, 2 letters, interview 5/8/93. That is his photo (from 1951) on the cover.

NON-PLAYERS WHO HELPED

Jim Gallagher, traveling secretary/alumni relations, Philadelphia Eagles (Gallagher retired in 1995.)
Joe Horrigan, librarian, NFL Hall of Fame and his staff
Dino Lucarelli, player relations/media services, Cleveland Browns
Doug Green, assistant director of public relations, Chicago Bears
Chris Tomasson, staff writer, Akron Beâcon-Journal
Jeannie H. Speedie, widow of Mac Speedie (1946-1952)
Mike Grgich, son of Visco Grgich (1946-1952)
Michael Connors, Assistant Director Sports Information, University of Nevada
Jean M. Elliott, Director of Sports Information, College of William and Mary
Don Tomkalski, Sports Information Director, Tulsa University
NFL Alumni, Fort Lauderdale, Fla.

BOOKS

Two books on this list deserve special mention: the one by Dan Daly & Bob O'Donnell and the one by Paul Zimmerman. I used both extensively for background information, particularly in the early chapters. Daly & O'Donnell provided particularly useful information on race, on scandals, and on the economics of the sport. Zimmerman's book (and Tom Bennett's) provided great insight into strategy, among other things. The late Paul Brown is quoted extensively; many of those remarks come from his autobiography. Most of the information on early TV coverage comes from the Patton book.

Allen, George, with Olan, Ben. *Pro Football's 100 Greatest Players.* The Bobbs-Merrill Company. Indianapolis/New York. 1982.

Bennett, Tom. *The Pro Style–The Complete Guide to Understanding National Football League Strategy.* Prentice-Hall. Englewood Cliffs, N.J. 1976.

Brown, Lloyd. *The Young Paul Robeson–"On My Journey Now."* Westview Press. Boulder, Colo. 1997.

Brown, Paul, with Clary, Jack. *PB: The Paul Brown Story.* Atheneum Publishers. New York. 1979

Campbell, Donald P. *Sunday's Warriors: The Philadelphia Eagles' History.* Quantum Leap. Philadelphia. 1994.

Carroll, John. *Fritz Pollard.* University of Illinois Press. Urbana and Chicago. 1992.

Claassen, Harold. *Ronald Encyclopedia of Football.* The Ronald Press Company. New York. 1961.

Cope, Myron. *The Game That Was–The Early Days of Pro Football.* The World Publishing Company. New York and Cleveland. 1970.

Daly, Dan and O'Donnell, Bob. *The Pro Football Chronicle.* Collier Books/ MacMillan Publishing Company. New York. 1990.

Danzig, Allison. *The History of American Football.* Prentice-Hall. Englewood Cliffs, N.J.. 1956.

—*Oh How They Played The Game–The Early Days of Football and The Heroes Who Made It Great.* MacMillan. New York. 1971.

Donovan, Arthur Jr. and Bob Drury. *Fatso–Football When Men Were Really Men*. Avon Books. New York. 1988.

Duroska, Lud, editor. *Great Pro Running Backs*. Grosset & Dunlap. New York. 1973.

Falkner, David. *Great Time Coming–The Life of Jackie Robinson From Baseball to Birmingham*. Touchstone. New York. 1995.

Faurot, Don. *"Football Secrets of the 'Split-T' Formation*. Prentice-Hall. Englewood Cliffs, N.J. 1956.

The First Fifty Years–A Celebration of the National Football League in its Fiftieth Season. Simon and Schuster. New York. 1969.

Furlow, Herbert M. *1980–The Pocket Book of Pro Football*. Pocket Books. New York. 1980.

Greenberg, Hank with Ira Berkow, *The Story of My Life*. Times Books. New York. 1989.

Herskowitz, Mickey. *The Golden Age of Pro Football*. Taylor Publishing Company. Dallas. 1990.

Horrigan, Joe. *The Official Pro Football Hall of Fame Answer Book*. Little Simon. New York. 1990.

Hyman, Mervin D., and White, Gordon S. Jr. *Big Ten Football–Its Life and Times, Great Coaches, Players and Games*. MacMillan. New York. 1977.

Kaplan, Richard. *Great Upsets of the NFL*. Random House. New York. 1972.

Korch, Rick. *The Truly Great. The 200 Best Pro Football Players of All Time*. Taylor Publishing Company. Dallas. 1993.

Kuklick, Bruce. *To Every Thing a Season. Shibe Park and Urban Philadelphia 1909-1976*. Princeton University Press. Princeton, N.J. 1991.

Landry, Tom and Lewis, Gregg. *Tom Landry–An Autobiography*. Harper Paperbacks. New York. 1990.

Leckie, Robert. *The Story of Football*. Random House. New York. 1971.

Leuthner, Stuart. *Iron Men–Bucko, Crazylegs, and the Boys Recall the Golden Days of Professional Football*. Doubleday. New York. 1988.

Levene, Peter. *Ellis Island to Ebbets Field–Sport and the American Jewish Experience*. Oxford University Press. New York. 1992.

Marshall, William. *Baseball's Pivotal Era, 1945-1951*. The University

Press of Kentucky. Lexington, Ky. 1999.

McCallum, John D. & Pearson, Charles H. *College Football U.S.A. 1869-1971.* Hall of Fame Publishing Inc. 1972.

Michael, Paul. *Professional Football's Greatest Games.* Prentice-Hall. Englewood Cliffs, N.J. 1972.

NCAA Football's Finest. The National Collegiate Athletic Association. Overland Park, Kan. 1991.

Neft, David S.; Johnson, Roland T.; Cohen, Richard, M.; and Deutsch, Jordan A. *The Sports Encyclopedia. Pro Football.* Grosset & Dunlap. New York. 1974.

Neft, David S.; Cohen, Richard M.; and Korch, Rick. *The Football Encylopedia.* St. Martin's Press. New York. 1994.

Newhouse, Dave. *Heismen–After The Glory.* The Sporting News Publishing Co. St. Louis. 1985.

NFL's Official Encyclopedic History of Professional Football, The. MacMillan Publishing Co. New York. 1977.

Official National Football League 1991 Record & Fact Book, The. Workman Publishing Co. New York. 1991.

Official 1993 NCAA Football. The National Collegiate Athletic Association. Overland Park, Kan. 1993.

Olderman, Murray. *The Running Backs.* Prentice-Hall. Englewood Cliffs, N.J. 1969

Patton, Phil. *Razzle-Dazzle–The Curious Marriage of Television & Football.* Dial Press. Garden City, N.Y.. 1984.

Porter, David L., editor. *Biographical Dictionary of American Sports. Football.* Greenwood Press. New York. 1987

Riffenburgh, Beau. *The Official NFL Encyclopedia.* New American Library. New York. 1986.

Roberts, Howard. *The Story of Pro Football.* Rand McNally & Company. New York. 1953

Shanklin, Bill. *Against All Odds–Football's Great Comebacks & Upsets.* Barclay House. New York. 1994.

Smith, Michael. *Illustrated History of Pro Football.* Madison Square Press. New York. 1970.

Smith, Red. *The Red Smith Reader.* edited by Dave Anderson. Vintage

Books. New York. 1983.

Strode, Woody, and Young, Sam. *Goal Dust–The Warm and Candid Memoirs of a Pioneer Black Athlete and Actor.* Madison Books. Lanham, Md. 1990.

Sullivan, George. *Pro Football's All-Time Greats.* G.P. Putnam's Sons. New York. 1968.

--*Pro Football A to Z.* Winchester Press. New York. 1975

Superstars of Autumn–75 years of the NFL's Greatest Players. Turner Publishing Inc. Atlanta. 1994

Thorn, John, editor. *The Armchair Quarterback.* Charles Scribner's Sons. New York. 1982. Writers included Bob Braunwart, Bob Carroll, Jack Cusack, Dave Anderson and Joe Horrigan.

Treat, Roger. *The Official National Football League Football Encyclopedia.* A&S Barnes & Co. New York. 1952.

Tunnell, Emlen. *Footsteps of a Giant.* Doubleday & Company. Garden City, N.Y.. 1966.

Vass, George. *George Halas and the Chicago Bears.* Henry Regency Company. Chicago. 1971.

Weinstein, Stephen. *The Random House Pro Football Dictionary.* Random House. New York. 1993.

The World Almanac, 1993 and successive editions

Zimmerman, Paul. *The New Thinking Man's Guide to Pro Football.* Simon and Schuster. New York. 1984.

ALSO IN PRINT

I did extensive research in the libraries of the two newspapers that employed me during the last decade, The Philadelphia Inquirer and The Record of Hackensack, N.J. This is a listing of some of the more important articles that I used.

Unless otherwise stated, all wire-service accounts that are cited in the text appeared in print on the day after the specific game or incident occurred; most of those news accounts are not listed below.

As a newspaper editor, I sometimes saw articles that were sent out for publication but may not have been published immediately or at all.

In those cases, when listing an article, I used the date that the article was sent out for publication and identified by whom.

Ambler, Neil "Emlen Tunnell, Dies; Star of Football Giants." *The New York Times.* 7/24/75. Page 32.

Anastasia, Phil. "Eagles Glory Years." *The Courier-Post*, Cherry Hill, N.J., 10/30/88. Page 8E.

Arizona Cardinals media guide, 1997

The Associated Press. "Coaches' Bloodlines Run Deep." Published in *The Record.* Hackensack, N.J. 8/25/91.

--"Kids Came First for Football Legend." Published in *The Record.* Hackensack, N.J. 8/8/91.

Berry, Mort. "Browns Win But Don't Gloat; Bell Praises Coach, Team." *The Philadelphia Inquirer.* 9/17/50.

--"Browns' Speedie One of Best Pass-Catching Wingmen." *The Philadelphia Inquirer.* 9/12/50.

--"Browns' Ford May Be Pihos' Equal." *The Philadelphia Inquirer.* 8/30/50.

--"Browns' Gillom Bodes Woe for Eagles Here Sept. 16." *The Philadelphia Inquirer.* 8/19/50.

--"Browns' Lavelli Learned Defensive Art by Watching." *The Philadelphia Inquirer.* 8/15/50.

Bowman football cards. 1948 and 1950 series. (reprints used)

Brady, Erik. "Pioneer Found Pain, Not Fame in Pro Football" *USA Today.* 9/20/95. Page C1.

Brown, Hugh. "Business Before Pleasure for Pihos." *The Philadelphia Evening Bulletin.* 12/4/55.

Chicago Bears media guides, 1992-1993, 1997

Cleveland Browns media guides, 1993-1994

Dufresne, Chris. "Ex-Ram Tom Fears Shows Alzheimer's Symptoms, but Doesn't Want Pity. *The Los Angeles Times.* Transmitted by Washington Post/Los Angeles Times News Service on 9/17/94.

Del Greco, Al. "For the Record." *The Bergen Evening Record.* Hackensack, N.J., 9/22/49. Page 24.

Didinger, Ray. "Championship Had Lighter Side." *The Philadelphia Daily News*. 4/16/94. Page 80.

—"Jimmy G" *The Philadelphia Daily News.* Transmitted by Knight-Ridder News Service 8/29/95.

—"The Best Team of the Best Years." Article in NFL game programs, 1987

—"'Wojie' dies at age 76." *The Philadelphia Daily News*. 7/14/92. Page 67.

—"Van Buren nearly a snow-show for title." *The Philadelphia Daily News.* 11/2/94. Page 78.

—"50 years ago, Marion Motley helped break down football's color barrier." *The Philadelphia Daily News.* Transmitted by Knight-Ridder News Service. 10/19/95

Edson, Bill. "Profile. Leon Cook." *The Enid Morning News.* Enid, Okla. 5/25/86. Pages E1, E3.

"Eagles Bonus Beauty." Eagles game program. Eagles vs. College All-Stars. 8/12/49. Pages 16, 19.

Feola, Lyn. "40 Years After, Fame Came Due." *The Record.* Hackensack, N.J. 9/17/89.

Fitzpatrick, Frank. "A placekicking king in high-tops." *The Philadelphia Inquirer.* 12/1/00. Page D8.

Goldstein, Herman. "Browns Near Second Title on Speed, Instead of Power." *The Sporting News*. 11/26/47. Section 2, Page 7.

Green Bay Packers media guide, 1997

Hawkins, Stephen. "Conerly remembered; trophy established in his Honor." Associated Press. Transmitted for publication 5/13/96.

Hogan, Ed. "Weavin Steven." Eagles game program, Eagles vs. Cardinals, 10/8/49. Page 5.

Jeffrey, Bob. "The Saga of The Reedville Strong Boy." *W&M Alumni Gazette*. June 1990. Page 6.

Life Magazine. "Notre Dame: Best Team in the Nation Gets Into Shape for Another Stiff Season. 9/29/47. Pages 86-91.

—"Southern Methodist: It has Halfback Doak Walker and Great Expectations. 9/27/48. Pages 79-87.

Lyghtle, Dave. "GRGICH. Original 49er Can't Be Copied." *The Modesto Bee.* Modesto, Calif. 10/8/86. Pages C1, C7.

Lyon, Bill. "Eagles' lineup takes a big hit." *The Philadelphia Inquirer.* 7/27/95. Page D-1.

Morgan Jr., David Lee. "Great player, good man." *The Akron Beacon Journal.* Akron, Ohio. 8/7/99.

—"Gillom's legend rose above punts." *The Akron Beacon Journal.* Akron, Ohio. 7/15/99.

Murray, Ken. "Tank Younger's NFL Success Opened Doors for Others." *The Batlimore Sun.* Transmitted by Washington Post/Los Angeles Times News Service on 2/18/93.

Newhouse, Dave. "Yesterday's Heroes." San Francisco 49ers game program. 1/2/83. Page 13C

O'Gara, Frank. "Barnes Tackled Bears in '48, Shot at One Near Grid Camp." *The Philadelphia Inquirer.* 9/6/49.

—"Tommyhawk Tommy." Game program, Eagles vs. College All-Stars, 8/12/49. Pages 6-7.

Philadelphia Eagles media guides, 1989 and successive years.

Pluto, Terry. "The Toe: Groza Much More Than a Kicker. The Akron Beacon Journal. Transmitted by Knight-Ridder News Service on 4/11/96.

—"Browns Reunion With Fans Shows How It Was Meant To Be. Akron Beacon Journal. Transmitted by Knight-Ridder News Service on 7/14/96.

Robinson, Alan. "Remembering When the Eagles and Steelers Were Teammates." Article written for The Associated Press for publication 12/4/93.

Seaburn, John. "Better Idea for Browns' Ford." *The Akron Beacon Journal.* Akron, Ohio. 7/21/99.

—"Answering the Call for a Doctor." *The Akron Beacon Journal.* Akron, Ohio. 6/30/99.

—"Gatski: At the Center of Browns' Early Years. *The Akron Beacon Journal.* Akron, Ohio. 8/21/99.

Seltzer, Robert. "Tommy Thompson Dies." *The Philadelphia Inquirer.* 4/22/89. Page C1.

Sports Illustrated. Special NFL Classic Edition. Fall 1995

Springer, Steve. "History Shows L.A. Market Fickle, Fertile for Football." *Los Angeles Times.* Transmitted by Washington Post/Los Angeles Times News Service on 2/4/96.

Stellino, Vito. "In Any Era, Don Hutson Would Have Been a Standout." *The Baltimore Sun.* Transmitted by Washington Post/Los Angeles Times News Service on 6/28/97.

Weimers, Leigh. "Al Ruffo was present at the creation of one of football's best franchises." Transmitted by Knight-Ridder News Service on 11/19/96.

Printed in the United States
728000001B